MALIKA™

Warrior Queen

MALIKA™

Warrior Queen

VOLUME ONE

CREATOR AND WRITER **ROYE OKUPE**

ART **CHIMA KALU**

COLORS **RAPHAEL KAZEEM**

WITH COLOR ASSISTANCE FROM
OSAS ASEMOTO, COLLINS MOMODU, OMOTUYI EBOTA, AND STANLEY NWEKE

LETTERS **SPOOF ANIMATION**

COVER ART AND BREAK PAGE 148 **GODWIN AKPAN**

MING DYNASTY CONCEPT ART
KAIJU DEN LLP (SINGAPORE), LESLIE NG KAZUKI, CHYI MING LEE, AARON LIN, AND WILLY WONG

LOGO DESIGN AND "MAP OF AZZAZ" **PAUL LOUISE-JULIE**

YOUNEEK EDITIONS EDITOR **AYODELE ELEGBA**

DARK HORSE BOOKS

Publisher **Mike Richardson**

Senior Editor **Philip R. Simon**

Associate Editor **Judy Khuu**

Assistant Editor **Rose Weitz**

Designer **Kathleen Barnett**

Digital Art Technician **Adam Pruett**

MALIKA: WARRIOR QUEEN VOLUME 1

This volume features all story pages from *Malika: Warrior Queen* Volumes 1 and 2 (published by YouNeek Studios in 2017 and 2018) with completely remastered and re-lettered story pages, and also collects the one-shot stories "Malika: Dragon Trials" (2017) and "WindMaker: Birth of a King" (2018), originally published by YouNeek Studios.

Published by Dark Horse Books | A division of Dark Horse Comics LLC | 10956 SE Main Street | Milwaukie, OR 97222

DarkHorse.com

To find a comics shop in your area, visit comicshoplocator.com

Library of Congress Cataloging-in-Publication Data

Names: Okupe, Roye, writer. | Kalu, Chima, artist. | Kazeem, Raphael, colourist. | Spoof Animation, letterer. | Akpan, Godwin, cover artist.
Title: Malika : warrior queen / writer, Roye Okupe ; artist, Chima Kalu ; colors, Raphael Kazeem ; letters, Spoof Animation ; cover art, Godwin Akpan.
Description: Milwaukie, OR : Dark Horse Books, 2021.
Identifiers: LCCN 2021006009 | ISBN 9781506723082 (trade paperback)
Subjects: LCSH: Graphic novels.
Classification: LCC PN6727.O486 M35 2021 | DDC 741.5/973--dc23
LC record available at https://lccn.loc.gov/2021006009

First edition: September 2021
Ebook ISBN 978-1-50672-317-4
Paperback ISBN 978-1-50672-308-2

1 3 5 7 9 10 8 6 4 2

Printed in China

House of Bakwa Family Crest

Azzazian Imperial Crest

CHAPTER ONE

Empire of Azzaz

The empire of Azzaz is made up of five provinces, all of which surround the capital city at the center. Each province pays a tribute and as a result gets to elect a chief who both governs its people as well as represents them on the Council (commonly called "The Council of Five"). The Council, in turn, advises the ruler of Azzaz. Although not law, no Azzazian ruler can have absolute power over the Council.

TIMBUKTU
SONGHAY EMPIRE
KANO PROVINCE
EMPIRE OF AZZAZ
BORNU PROVINCE
FON PROVINCE
NUPE PROVINCE
CITY OF AZZAZ
MANDARA PROVINCE
MANDILA MOUNTAINS
AKAN REGION
OYO KINGDOM
CITY OF CONFLUENCE
BENIN KINGDOM
AWORI
GOLD COAST
NRI
N
W
E
S
KINGDOM OF ATALA
ORIS
RAVEN
MAP OF AZZAZ UNDER THE RULE OF QUEEN MALIKA
EST 1499 BC

ROYAL PALACE, CITY OF AZZAZ.
HA!
HA!
HAAAA!
MALIKA, WHERE DID YOU LEARN TO WIELD A DAGGER?

IT IS OKAY, CHILD. I AM NOT UPSET. IN FACT, I AM IMPRESSED.

EVERY MORNING, I SNEAK INTO THE ARENA TO WATCH THE SOLDIERS TRAIN.

WHEN I GET BACK, I TRY TO PRACTICE EVERYTHING.

IMPRESSIVE. AND HOW LONG HAVE YOU BEEN DOING THIS?

MMMM... ABOUT A YEAR OR SO.

YOU HAVE ALWAYS BEEN A CURIOUS ONE, HAVEN'T YOU? WELL, KEEP PRACTICING.

MAYBE YOU WILL MAKE A GREAT WARRIOR SOMEDAY.

VERY WELL. YOU HAVE TWO CAVALRY UNITS, SOME INFANTRY, AND SOME ARCHERS.

IN YOUR WAY IS A FORMIDABLE FOE WITH A HUGE NUMBER OF INFANTRY UNITS. WHAT DO YOU DO?

SIMPLE. I'D USE MY CAVALRY TO ATTACK BOTH FLANKS, MAKING THE ENEMY RAM INTO ONE ANOTHER AT THE CENTER.

THEN, I'D ORDER MY ARCHERS TO CONCENTRATE FIRE ON THEM DURING THE COMMOTION. THE REST IS QUITE EASY.

IMPRESSIVE... PERHAPS YOU WILL BE READY SOONER THAN I THOUGHT.

YES! FOR *AZZAZ!*

YOU WOULD MAKE A GREAT QUEEN, MY DEAR.

BUT... THAT IS NADIA'S BIRTHRIGHT.
OF COURSE. YOUR OLDER SISTER IS YOUR FATHER'S NATURAL CHOICE. HOWEVER, IN AZZAZ, SUCCESSION IS NOT SOLELY BASED ON AGE, BUT MERIT AS WELL.
THEN AGAIN, YOUR SISTER IS FORMIDABLE, SO YOU PROBABLY WILL NOT HAVE TO WORRY ABOUT THE BURDEN OF RULING.

ABDUL-NASSER HAS BEEN A TRUSTED ADVISER TO YOUR FATHER, THE KING, FOR YEARS. HE WILL HANDLE YOUR TRAINING HENCEFORTH.
YES, MOTHER.
WELL...GO ON THEN. KEEP PRACTICING.
SWIPE

QUEEN MALIKA, WE ARE ABOUT TEN KILOMETERS FROM THE BATTLEFIELD.
GOOD.
BORNU PROVINCE, EMPIRE OF AZZAZ.
RAAAR
ABDUL, TO THE RIGHT.
I SEE, MY QUEEN. BEST WE KEEP MOVING. NOTHING WE CAN DO FOR HIM NOW. WE NEED TO HURRY TO--
ABANDON A HELPLESS CHILD? THE CHIVALRY TRULY SHINES FROM WITHIN YOU, ABDUL.
MY QUEEN, IT IS BAD ENOUGH THAT YOU ARE ALL THE WAY OUT HERE.
IN THE FURTHEST REACHES OF YOUR EMPIRE. WE NEED TO FOCUS ON THE REBELS.

THE FURTHEST PART OF MY EMPIRE IS STILL MY EMPIRE. AND I WILL PROTECT ALL OF MY PEOPLE.
BESIDES, HIS KIND IS NOT THE ONE REBELLING AGAINST ME. IT IS MY GENERALS WHO CANNOT STAND TO SEE ME IN POWER...YOUR BOW.
NOT ALL YOUR GENERALS. SOME WILL FOLLOW YOU TO THE DEATH.
THOSE I KEEP CLOSE.

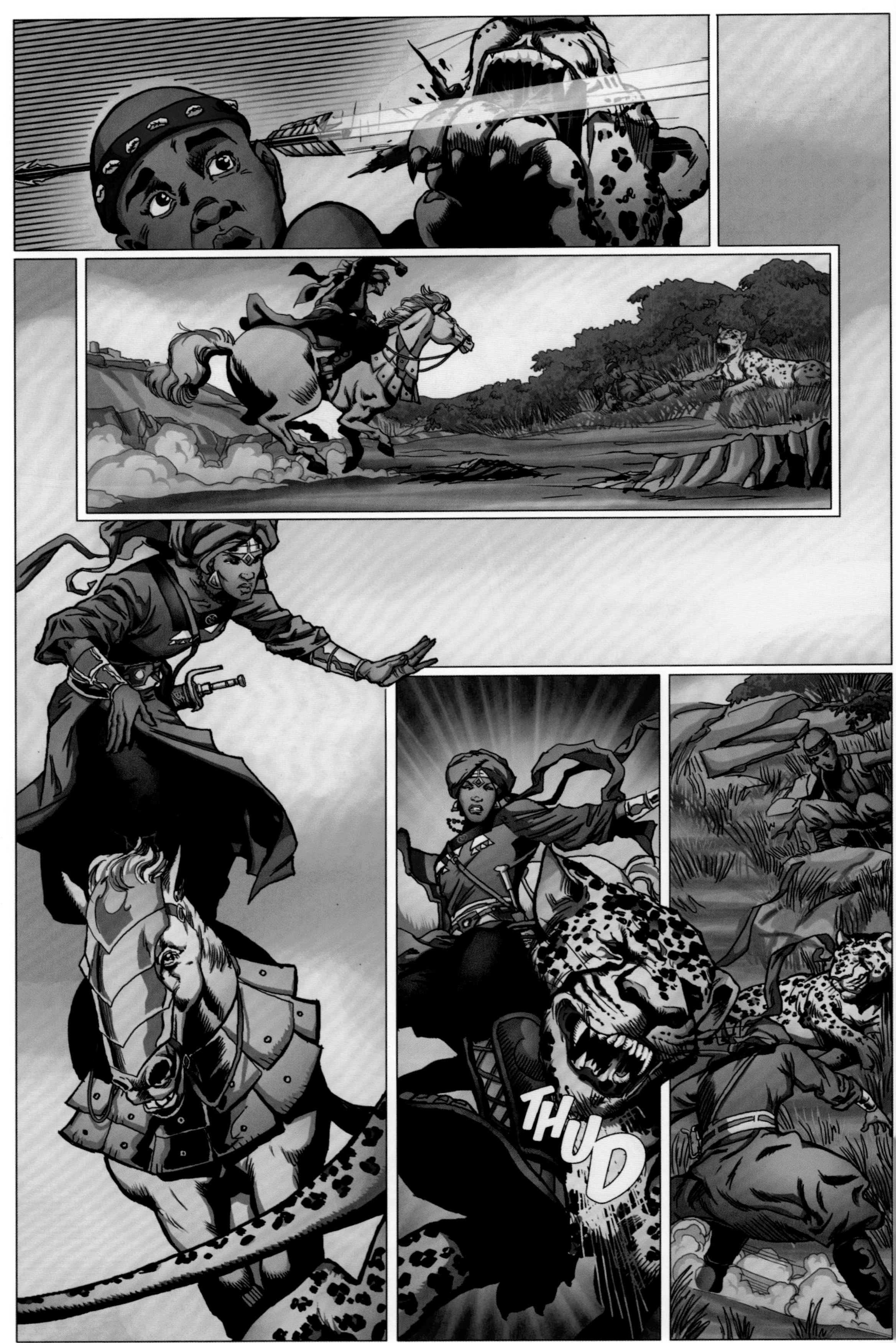
THUD

THANK YOU, MY QUEEN! THANK YOU!
RISE, LITTLE ONE. YOU ARE MOST WELCOME.
WHAT ARE YOU DOING ALL THE WAY OUT HERE? SURELY YOU KNOW HOW DANGEROUS THESE FIELDS ARE.
I WAS SEARCHING FOR FOOD, YOUR MAJESTY.
THE SIEGE... IT HAS MADE THE LOCALS DESPERATE.
MY PEOPLE ARE HUNGRY. AND THE REBELS, THE ONES WHO CALL THEMSELVES THE SAVIORS OF AZZAZ, HAVE MADE LIFE MISERABLE.
THEY PUNISH AND ENSLAVE ALL THOSE WHO DO NOT JOIN THEM. INCLUDING CHIEF HAZAR.
THAT ENDS TODAY. I DID NOT UNITE AZZAZ AFTER A DECADE OF CIVIL WAR JUST FOR A FEW YEARS OF RELATIVE PEACE.
GET ON A HORSE, YOUNG ONE. TODAY WE TAKE BACK YOUR CITY.

CITY OF BAGA, BORNU PROVINCE.
SAVIORS OF AZZAZ, THE MEN OF TYRANT QUEEN MALIKA ARE HOPELESS. SHALL WE DESTROY THEM?!
HOLD THE LINE, MEN! FORM A SHIELD WALL!
HOO!
HOO!
HOO!
OUR QUEEN! SHE APPROACHES. QUEEN MALIKA IS HERE!

ABDUL, LEFT FLANK.

MALIKA!
MALIKA!
MALIKA!

STEADY, YOU COWARDS!

MEN! REGROUP!
HOLD THE LINE, YOU IDIOTS!

ARCHERS! FIRE AT THEIR CENTER!

RIDERS, DISMOUNT!
CHARGE!

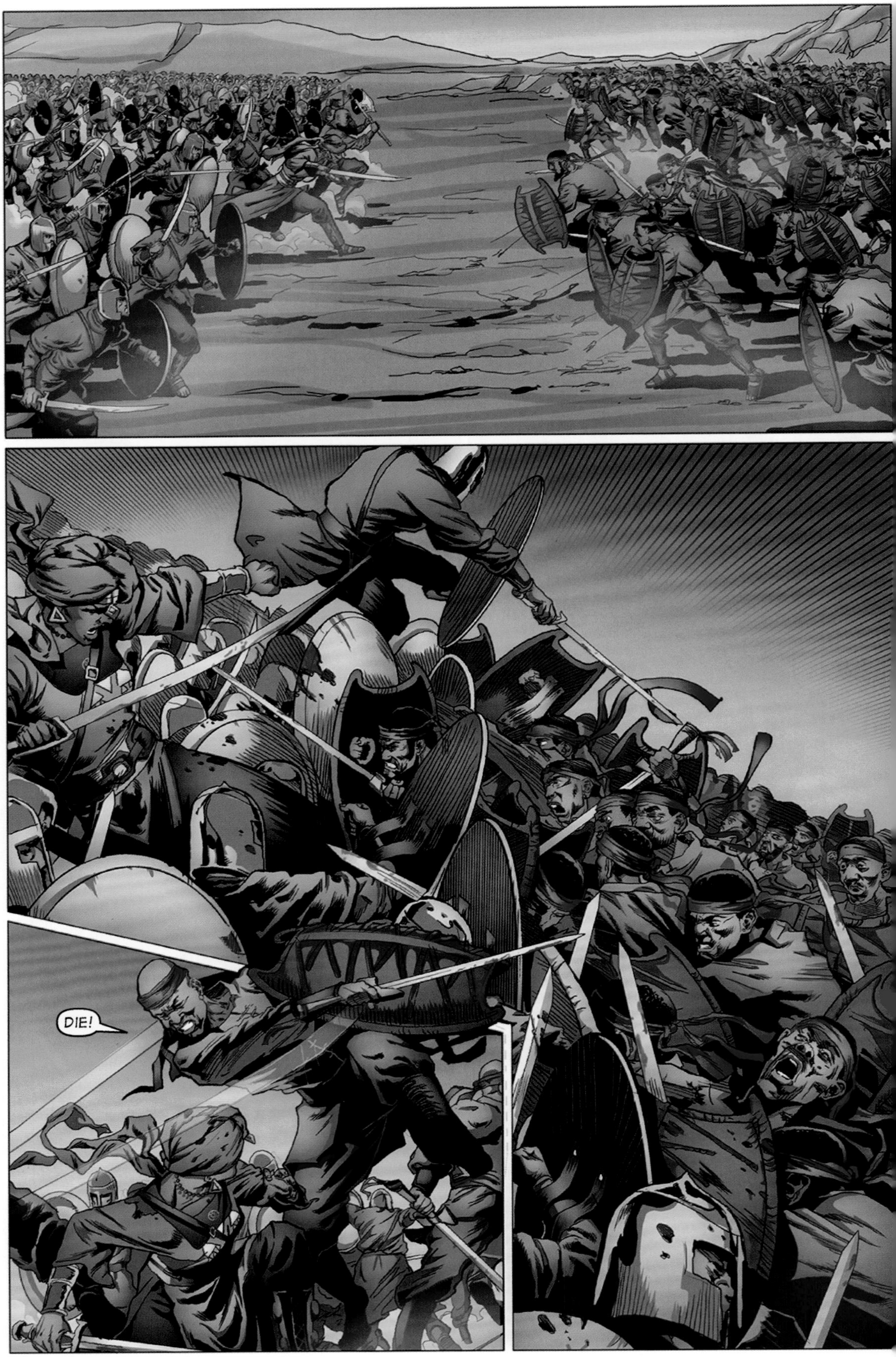

DIE!

CLANK
ARGH!
HAAAA!
HOLD!

COWARDS! STAND AND FIGHT! IF YOU FLEE I WILL KILL YOU MYSELF!
GENERAL RAS! IT IS CLEAR YOUR QUARREL IS WITH ME. LET US NOT INVOLVE INNOCENT AZZAZIANS IN THIS PETTY REBELLION.
PETTY? YOU DO NOT DESERVE THE THRONE. AFTER YOUR FATHER'S DEATH, IT WAS SUPPOSED TO GO TO YOUR UNCLE.
INSTEAD, YOUR MOTHER DIVIDED THE KINGDOM AFTER SHE ILLEGITIMATELY SEIZED THE THRONE.
YOU TRULY EXPECTED MY MOTHER TO TURN OVER MY FATHER'S KINGDOM TO MY UNCLE? THE MAN THEY CALLED BAKWA THE BUTCHER...
A MAN WHO KILLED WOMEN AND CHILDREN FOR HIS AMUSEMENT? THE SAME MAN THAT MURDERED MY FATHER FOR HIS THRONE?
THERE WAS NO PROOF. THE FACT REMAINS, IT WAS HIS RIGHT TO RULE.
HOW ABOUT WE JUST GET TO THE REAL REASON BEHIND YOUR REBELLION.
AN OVERSIZED CAMEL FACE LIKE YOU JUST DOESN'T LIKE BEING RULED BY A WOMAN.
YOU NEVER DID.
MAN OR WOMAN, YOUR RECKLESSNESS WITH THE ATALIANS CONFIRMED YOU ARE UNFIT TO RULE.
PROVE IT. I CHALLENGE YOU TO SINGLE COMBAT. PER OUR CUSTOMS, WHOMEVER WINS GETS THE OTHER PERSON'S TERRITORIES. NO NEED FOR ANY MORE AZZAZIAN BLOODSHED. YOU WIN, YOU ARE KING, I WIN, AND THIS REBELLION IS OVER.
MY QUEEN, I MUST OBJECT--
IT IS ALL RIGHT, ABDUL.

YOU JUST MADE THE BIGGEST MISTAKE OF YOUR MISERABLE LIFE...SELECT YOUR CHAMPION... "MY QUEEN."
I AM... MY CHAMPION...
DIE!
ARCHHH!
CRCKK
SLING

KRRAGGHHH!!

THE... SAVIOR... THE SAVIOR WILL DESTROY YOU...
MALIKA
SOMEONE PLEASE TAKE GENERAL RAS TO A HEALER BEFORE HE CHOKES ON HIS OWN BLOOD.
ALL HAIL QUEEN MALIKA! THE GREAT UNIFIER!
THE PROVINCE OF BORNU IS AT THE EDGE OF THIS EMPIRE, BUT YOU ARE STILL AZZAZIANS! AND EVERY AZZAZIAN DESERVES TO BE FREE.
YOU ALL KNOW ME TO BE A FAIR RULER, BUT I WILL NOT TOLERATE INSUBORDINATION.
ALL MEN AND WOMEN WHO PLEDGE THEIR ALLEGIANCE TO AZZAZ WILL BE SPARED AND THEIR CRIMES OF REBELLION FORGIVEN. I GIVE YOU MY WORD.
BUT IF YOU ARE NOT WITH ME, THEN YOU ARE AGAINST ME...WHICH ONE OF YOU STILL OPPOSES ME?
YOU COWARDS WOULD SO EASILY SURRENDER? SO BE IT...
THE REST OF US WILL STAY LOYAL TO THE SAVIOR'S CAUSE.
I URGE YOU TO RECONSIDER...YOU MEN ARE FULLY AWARE OF THE PENALTY OF TREASON.
ARE YOU WILLING TO PAY THE ULTIMATE PRICE FOR A SENSELESS REBELLION?
THE SAVIOR OF AZZAZ WILL AVENGE US!
VERY WELL.

CHAPTER TWO

Art by Godwin Akpan

THE BORNU PROVINCE

The Bornu Province, located in the Northeast just West of Lake Chad, provides the Azzazian Empire valuable access to Trans-Saharan trade routes. Chief Hazar currently governs the Bornu Province.

The fictional Bornu Province of Azzaz in *Malika: Warrior Queen* was inspired by the real-life Bornu Empire, which existed from 1380 to 1893. The historic Bornu Empire was located around the area of what is now Northeastern Nigeria.

SMALL VILLAGE, 700 KM SOUTHEAST OF AZZAZ.
PER YOUR REQUEST, GENERAL CHENG, WE HAVE GATHERED ALL THE ELDERS FROM OUR DIFFERENT TRIBES.
BOTH AS A SIGN OF RESPECT AND AS A PRECURSOR TO PEACEFUL NEGOTIATIONS.
FURTHERMORE, WE ASK THAT YOU ACCEPT THIS GENEROUS TRIBUTE AS A SIGN OF OUR COMMITMENT TOWARDS HARMONY WITH THE MING DYNASTY.
WE ASK HUMBLY FOR YOU TO DO AS WE AGREED...LEAVE OUR LANDS IN PEACE...
INDEED, THIS IS GENEROUS... AND YES, I DID AGREE TO "LEAVE YOU IN PEACE."
BUT, I NEVER ACTUALLY AGREED TO "LEAVE."
GENERAL CHENG! YOU CANNOT DO THIS! WE HAD AN AGREEMENT! HAVE YOU NO HONOR?!

HONOR IS OVERRATED... ARCHERS, GIVE THEM THE PEACE THEY REQUEST.
FIRE!
ARCHHH!
PLEASE, HAVE MERCY!
GENERAL...
THE SWORD... IT GLOWS. DOES THIS MEAN WE CAN FINALLY ACCESS ITS POWERS?
NO...IT MEANS SOMEONE WHO CAN MAY BE CLOSE...WE STICK TO THE PLAN. THE *DRAGON STONES* REMAIN THE PRIORITY.
HAVE THE MEN SET UP CAMP. AFTERWARDS, YOU WILL PERSONALLY DELIVER A *MESSAGE* TO QUEEN MALIKA.

THE CITY OF AZZAZ.

OPEN THE GATE!

PLEASE, TAKE YOUR SEATS. IT HAS BEEN TOO LONG SINCE THE COUNCIL GATHERED...
THE ISSUE WITH THESE REBELS, OR AS THEY CALL THEMSELVES, "THE SAVIORS OF AZZAZ," MUST BE CONTAINED. IT SEEMS MY DEAD *UNCLE* HAS MORE SYMPATHIZERS THAN I GAVE HIM CREDIT FOR. *BORNU* WILL NOT BE THE LAST.
QUEEN MALIKA! MANY THANKS FOR PERSONALLY RESCUING ME AND MY PROVINCE. I OWE YOU MY LIFE.
NO NEED FOR THANKS, CHIEF HAZAR. IT IS OUR DUTY TO PROTECT ONE ANOTHER.
PERHAPS WE WOULD NOT HAVE PROBLEMS WITH REBELS IF OUR QUEEN DID NOT AID THE KINGDOM OF ATALA! MANY AZZAZIANS DISAPPROVED OF OUR ARMY MARCHING AGAINST THE MING DYNASTY.

HOW DARE YOU, DOGBARI?! YOU WILL TREAT YOUR QUEEN WITH RESPECT!
AS CHIEF OF THE FON PROVINCE, I DESERVE TO HAVE MY SAY.
YOUR MAJESTY... I SIMPLY WAS POINTING OUT--
WHOEVER SAID I ASSISTED ATALA? I SIMPLY WENT ON A SPIRITUAL JOURNEY WITH MY ROYAL GUARDS.
BUT MY QUEEN, YOUR CAVALRY AND YOUR FEROCITY IN BATTLE... THEY ARE UNMISTAKABLE. NO ONE WAS FOOLED BY YOUR UNITS' DISGUISE.
AND NOW, AN EMISSARY OF MING IS HERE AND WE CANNOT HELP BUT THINK THAT THE INTERFERENCE WITH THE ATALIANS--
IS BEING USED AS AN EXCUSE TO DEFY MY RULE. SOMEONE IS BEHIND THESE REBELLIONS.
THOSE MEN WERE PROPERLY TRAINED AND EQUIPPED.
THEY ARE AZZAZIANS WHO ARE JUST CONCERNED ABOUT THE SAFETY OF THEIR FAMILIES.
I SAY WE SMOKE THEM OUT AND DESTROY EVERY SINGLE ONE OF THEM!
THEY ARE TRAITORS AND DESERVE TO BE TREATED AS SUCH!
PERHAPS YOU TOO ARE A TRAITOR, HAZAR. HOW DID YOU MANAGE TO SURVIVE AS A CAPTIVE OF THESE "MENACING" REBELS?
HOW DARE YOU, DOGBARI?! I WILL HAVE YOUR TONGUE FOR THAT!
I AGREE WITH DOGBARI! HAZAR, WHAT SECRETS DO YOU KEEP FROM US?
ENOUGH!

...I HAVE SEEN BETTER CONDUCT AT THE MARKET SQUARE... WE WILL DISCUSS THIS AT A LATER TIME.
GUARD, SEND IN THE EMISSARY.
QUEEN MALIKA, THE GREAT UNIFIER. LEADER OF THE FORMIDABLE FIVE. I AM COLONEL ZHANG.
I COME AS A HUMBLE MESSENGER OF GENERAL CHENG OF THE MING DYNASTY. TRUSTED ADVISER TO OUR GREAT EMPEROR.
SPEAK...
KING BASS KAZAAR, OR AS HE IS COMMONLY REFERRED TO, THE "WINDMAKER," ALONG WITH HIS RED RAVEN ARMY, ARE REBELS AND ENEMIES OF MING.
GENERAL CHENG HAS BEEN TASKED--
REBELS?
YOU MORE THAN ANYONE CAN APPRECIATE INTOLERANCE FOR INSUBORDINATION.

I TOOK BACK A KINGDOM THAT WAS FRACTURED BY CIVIL WAR. "MY" KINGDOM. YOUR PEOPLE INVADED ATALA.
KING BASS AND HIS MEN FOUGHT AND TOOK BACK THEIR LANDS.
THE ATALIAN UPRISING WAS JUST, AS WAS MY REUNIFICATION OF AZZAZ.
ALL A MATTER OF PERSPECTIVE, YOUR GRACE...BE THAT AS IT MAY, GENERAL CHENG HAS REQUESTED YOU USE YOUR RELATIONSHIP WITH THE ATALIANS TO...DO WHAT IS NECESSARY.
YOU MEAN KILL KING BASS...
WITHOUT THEIR KING AND HIS..."WIND POWERS," ATALA WILL FALL TO THE MING DYNASTY...
WE ARE WILLING TO FORGIVE YOUR MINOR INTERFERENCE. SURELY YOU DID NOT THINK WE WOULD NOT KNOW YOU HELPED THE ATALIANS.
AND IF I REFUSE THIS..."KIND" OFFER?
YOU AND YOUR EMPIRE WILL BE DESTROYED.
YOU WILL WATCH YOUR TONGUE, PEASANT, OR I SHALL CUT IT OUT AND FEED IT TO THE DOGS.

I DO NOT RESPOND VERY WELL TO THREATS.

I AM MERELY A MESSENGER, YOUR GRACE.

SEND WORD TO KING BASS. TELL HIM THE QUEEN WOULD LIKE HIM TO BE HER HONORED GUEST ON ***UNIFICATION DAY.***

YES, MY QUEEN.

YOU MADE THE RIGHT CHOICE...

Art by Chima Kalu, with colors by Raphael Kazeem

CHAPTER THREE

Art by Godwin Akpan

The Fon Province

The Fon Province is located to the West of the city of Azzaz. Its access to rare raw materials like gold and ivory make it the richest of the Five Provinces. Chief Dogbari currently governs the Fon Province.

The Fon Province in this graphic novel was inspired by the real-life Fon people, whose history is linked to the Dahomey Kingdom. Located in a region that is now present-day Benin, the African Dahomey Kingdom existed from about 1600 to 1894.

AWORI, OYO KINGDOM.
RAVENS! ATTACK!
CLANG
ARGH!

HA!
SURROUND HIM!

WHOOSH
WHOOSH
WHOOSH
WHOOSH

MOMENTS LATER...
MY KING...
THE PRISONERS....
LET THESE MEN GO. THEY ARE NO THREAT TO US NOW.
BUT, MY KING--
THAT WILL BE ALL, BENGU.
YES, MY KING.
THANK YOU, YOUR GRACE.
I SPARED YOUR LIFE. NOW YOU MUST DO SOMETHING FOR ME IN RETURN. WHERE IS YOUR *GENERAL?*
GENERAL CHENG HAS MADE CAMP ABOUT SIX HUNDRED KILOMETERS EAST.
HE INSTRUCTED US TO AMBUSH YOU AND SLOW YOUR ADVANCE WHILE HE GATHERS REINFORCEMENTS FROM MING.

COWARD, HE HAS BEEN ON THE RUN EVER SINCE WE CHASED HIM OUT OF ATALA. HOW MANY REINFORCEMENTS?
MORE THAN YOU CAN EVER IMAGINE. HE IS ASSEMBLING THE *LARGEST* ARMY EVER ALLOWED OUTSIDE MING TERRITORY. IT IS RUMOURED TO BE FIVE TIMES THE SIZE OF THE ENTIRE AZZAZIAN ARMY.
WE SHALL SEE...
MY KING! A MESSAGE FROM AZZAZ.
SPEAK...
YOU HAVE BEEN INVITED TO AZZAZ AS THE QUEEN'S HONORED GUEST FOR THEIR UNIFICATION DAY.
ANYTHING ELSE?
NO, MY KING.
VERY WELL. BENGU, INFORM THE RED KNIGHTS I DEPART WITH THEM AT FIRST LIGHT. I LEAVE YOU IN CHARGE OF THE ARMY.
THE ARMY IS NOT TRAVELING WITH YOU?
NO. MOVE THE MEN EAST OF THE *CITY OF CONFLUENCE* AND AWAIT MY INSTRUCTIONS.
BUT MY KING--
DO NOT ARGUE, BENGU. DO AS YOU ARE TOLD.

YOU FOUGHT BRAVELY TODAY, LITTLE SISTER.
OF COURSE I DID. ONE OF US HAD TO.
YOU ARE NEVER LACKING FOR CONFIDENCE, ARE YOU?
WELL...WHEN YOU BECOME QUEEN, MY CONFIDENCE WILL COME IN HANDY...
PRINCESS MALIKA, PRINCESS NADIA, WE ARE HONORED THAT YOU HAVE GRACED US WITH YOUR PRESENCE.
QUIT THE PLEASANTRIES. YOU KNOW WHY WE ARE HERE.

I CAN ASSURE YOU OUR PEOPLE HAD NOTHING TO DO WITH THE ATTACK ON YOUR MEN. THOSE WERE YOUR UNCLE'S SYMPATHIZERS.
PROVE IT. PLEDGE YOUR ALLEGIANCE TO MY MOTHER, THE RIGHTFUL RULER OF ALL OF AZZAZ. CHOOSE OTHERWISE, AND THIS WILL BE THE LAST DAY YOU WALK THE EARTH.
NADIA, WHAT ARE YOU DOING? MOTHER HAS SAID--
STAY OUT OF THIS, MALIKA! THIS IS WHAT THESE PEOPLE UNDERSTAND.
PRINCESS NADIA, YOU KNOW OUR PEOPLE ARE FORBIDDEN TO TAKE SIDES IN THIS CIVIL WAR.
INDECISION IS PRECISELY WHAT HAS DIVIDED THIS KINGDOM. MEN, LET US SHOW THEM WHAT HAPPENS TO TRAITORS!
NADIA, THIS IS MADNESS! THESE PEOPLE ARE INNOCENT.
NO THEY ARE NOT! DO YOU NOT SEE? I AM DOING THIS FOR OUR MOTHER. PEOPLE NEED TO FEAR US. THIS IS THE ONLY WAY.
AND YOU WILL NEVER SPEAK OF THIS TO HER. UNDERSTOOD?

NADIA! WHAT HAVE YOU DONE?!
YOU TOLD HER?! HOW COULD YOU BETRAY ME?
NADIA! NO!!!
HOLD ON! PLEASE! JUST HOLD ON!
NADIA!!!!!

YOU WOULD HAVE MADE A BETTER QUEEN...

I FEAR THAT WHAT I AM ABOUT TO DO, I MAY REGRET.

YOU TAUGHT THEM BOTH, DID YOU NOT?
I PRACTICALLY RAISED THEM...
I DO NOT UNDERSTAND. IF THE RUMORS ARE TRUE, WHY BUILD A STATUE FOR NADIA? HER DEATH WAS--
--I SHALL... JUST...BE QUIET, SIR.
HAS HE ARRIVED?
EHH...AHHH...YES, MY QUEEN. KING BASS IS HERE. HE AWAITS YOUR PRESENCE IN THE THRONE ROOM.
GOOD... SHALL WE?

MY QUEEN, I GIVE YOU THE WINDMAKER, KING BASS OF ATALA.
QUEEN MALIKA. THE GREAT UNIFIER. LEGENDARY COMMANDER. YOU HAVE HONORED ATALA BY INVITING HER KING! AND I AM PERSONALLY GRATEFUL TO BE IN YOUR PRESENCE.
HMMM... I SEE THE RUMORS ABOUT YOUR FLATTERY ARE TRUE.
ALLOW ME TO PRESENT YOU WITH A GIFT.

FORGIVE MY FIRST MINISTER. ABDUL HAS WATCHED OVER ME ALL MY LIFE. I AM UNDEFEATED IN BATTLE, YET HE TREATS ME AS IF I AM STILL LEARNING TO CRAWL.
ABDUL, IF THE ATALIANS WANTED TO ASSASSINATE ME, I THINK THEY WOULD BE MUCH MORE DISCRETE.
AND WHAT MIGHT THIS BE?
THE LEGENDARY DRAGON'S DESTINY.
THE SWORD THAT IS SAID TO CONTAIN THE POWER OF ANCIENT DRAGONS? IT ACTUALLY EXISTS?
YES. IT WAS KEPT HIDDEN IN ATALA FOR CENTURIES.
THE ONLY DIFFERENCE BETWEEN TRUTH AND MYTHOLOGY IS--
A MYTHICAL SWORD...POWERED BY MYTHICAL CREATURES... THIS IS YOUR PRIZED POSSESSION?
FACTS...
LEGEND SAYS NO ONE HAS EVER BEEN ABLE TO ACTIVATE ITS POWERS.

THE WEAPON HOLDS THE QUINTESSENCE OF THE DIVINE ONES. ONLY A WARRIOR OF TRUE CLASS MAY HARNESS ITS POWERS.
I CAN THINK OF NO ONE MORE WORTHY THAN YOU.
CLINNN
"THE DOOM OF DARKNESS MUST YIELD TO THE LIGHT OF THE PERFECT WARRIOR."
SHALL WE FIND OUT?
JUST AS EXPECTED. AN ANTIQUE.

WELL, IT IS FANCY ENOUGH TO ADD TO MY COLLECTION OF TROPHIES. I ACCEPT YOUR GIFT, KING BASS, EVEN THOUGH IT FELL SHORT OF EXPECTATIONS.
MY APOLOGIES. I ASSUMED IF ANYONE COULD ACTIVATE ITS POWERS, IT WOULD BE YOU.
PERHAPS I AM JUST NOT AS WORTHY AS YOU THINK?
QUITE THE OPPOSITE...
WE HAVE PREPARED SPECIAL CHAMBERS FOR YOU AND YOUR MEN. YOU MUST BE EXHAUSTED FROM YOUR JOURNEY.
YOU SHOULD REST, FOR TOMORROW WE CELEBRATE. THANK YOU, EVERYONE.
VERY WELL...
I HAVE A MAN READY TO TAKE CARE OF THINGS.
I WILL DO IT MYSELF.
MALIKA, PLEASE LET ME HANDLE THIS.
NO...I WILL NOT LET ANY OF MY PEOPLE HAVE THIS KIND OF BLOOD ON THEIR HANDS.
UNDERSTOOD...

WHAT IS IT?
NOTHING. I THOUGHT I HEARD SOMETHING.
CRCK
CRCK

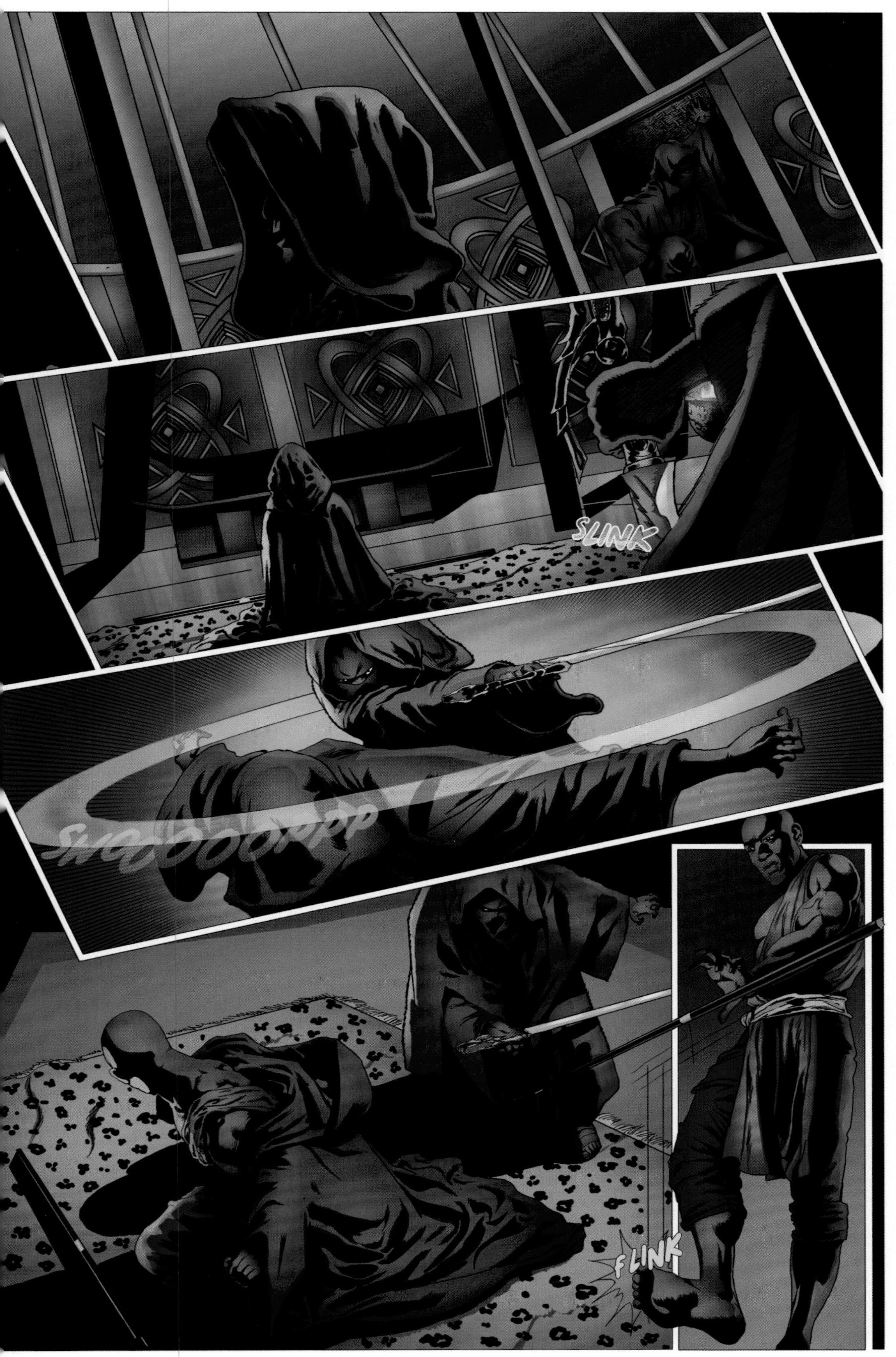
SLINK
SWOOOOOOPPP
FLINK

CLING
WHEEEM
SWIPPEE
THUD

BARK
IT SEEMS YOUR ROBES ARE SLOWING YOU DOWN...
...SO HOW ABOUT YOU JUST SHOW YOURSELF!
SHRRAAA

THUD
YOU HAVE GOTTEN SLOW, BASS...
SLINK

PLANNING TO KILL ME WITH MY GIFT?
WELL...MAYBE THE RUMORS ABOUT ME ARE TRUE.
ABOUT YOU KILLING ALL YOUR LOVERS AFTER ONE NIGHT?
THAT WOULD BE THE ONE...
...WELL, ARE YOU NOT?
WOULDN'T I HAVE TO BE YOUR LOVER FOR THAT TO HAPPEN?
I AM NOT YOUR LOVER. I AM YOUR HUSBAND...

WHAT TOOK YOU SO LONG?
I TRAINED THESE GUARDS. GETTING PAST THEM WAS NO EASY TASK.
I HAVE WATCHED THE SUN SET EVERY DAY SINCE I LAST SAW YOUR FACE...
...AND STILL, EACH TIME, IT PALES IN COMPARISON TO YOUR BEAUTY...I HAVE MISSED YOU SO MUCH, MY LOVE.
AS I, YOU. BUT WE HAVE MUCH TO DISCUSS. AND VERY LITTLE TIME.
AGREED.
SO...WAR WITH THE MING DYNASTY THEN?
NOT UNLESS YOU CAN BLOW THEIR ENTIRE ARMY TO OBLIVION.
YOU KNOW MY POWERS HAVE LIMITS.
I KNOW, MY LOVE. BESIDES, CHENG HAS SEEN ENOUGH TO HAVE COUNTER MEASURES READY FOR SUCH A DIRECT ATTACK.
I COULD SURRENDER MYSELF.
YOU KNOW I CANNOT LET THAT HAPPEN, BASS. BESIDES, THIS IS MORE THAN JUST ATALA NOW.
I HEARD...

CHENG HAS DESTROYED ENOUGH VILLAGES, BASS. HE SLAUGHTERS OUR NEIGHBORS WITH IMPUNITY. HIS AIM IS CONQUEST, NOT UNITY.
EVENTUALLY, HE WILL SET HIS EYES ON AZZAZ.
MAYBE SO. BUT HIS ARMY IS AT ITS LARGEST SINCE HE SAILED TO THIS CONTINENT...
WE WILL FIND A WAY. FORCE, STRENGTH, AND AGGRESSION. THIS IS WHAT WE AZZAZIANS KNOW BEST.
AN IRON FIST MAY HAVE UNITED YOUR KINGDOM, BUT IT WILL TAKE A GENTLE HAND TO PREVENT DIVISION...OR REBELLION.
FORCE IS THE ONLY THING AZZAZIANS RESPOND TO.
YOU CANNOT THREATEN WAR TO MAINTAIN PEACE. SOMETIMES YOU NEED TO SHOW THE SIDES OF YOU THAT ONLY I SEE.
LOVE, MERCY, FORGIVENESS...
SHOW THESE TO YOUR DETRACTORS, EVEN WHEN THEY SHOW YOU THE OPPOSITE.
I WILL NOT DISPLAY WEAKNESS!
YOU THINK LOVE IS WEAKNESS? IS THAT WHY YOU HAVE KEPT US A SECRET? OUR MARRIAGE MAKES YOU "WEAK"?

BASS, THAT WAS NOT...
BASS, I HAVE NOT SEEN YOU IN A WHILE. THE LAST THING I WANT FOR US IS TO FIGHT.
LET US DEAL WITH MING FIRST. THEN WE CAN DISCUSS MY FLAWS AS A RULER.
VERY WELL...
NOW, TELL ME WHY YOU REALLY BROUGHT THIS TO ME.
CHENG WAS ABLE TO GET HIS HANDS ON A SIMILAR WEAPON...DRAGON'S DOOM. HE CANNOT HAVE BOTH.
THERE IS A PLACE WITHIN THE MOUNTAINS AT THE CITY OF CONFLUENCE.
FEW KNOW THE LOCATION. IT WILL BE SAFE THERE.
WAR WITH MING IS SUICIDE. THEIR ARMY IS IN THE MILLIONS.
YES...BUT ARE WE FIGHTING MING? OR JUST CHENG?
STILL, WITH HIS REINFORCEMENTS, CHENG'S FORCES COULD EASILY BE FIVE TIMES OUR COMBINED NUMBERS.
VICTORY HAS NEVER ELUDED ME...AND IT WILL NOT START NOW.

HALL OF HASAN,
CITY OF AZZAZ.

IS IT DONE?
I DID WHAT WAS BEST FOR AZZAZ...

CITIZENS OF AZZAZ, I TRULY FEEL HONORED TO BE SURROUNDED BY YOU TONIGHT.
FOR ON THIS DAY, TEN YEARS AGO, WE CELEBRATED THE UNIFICATION OF OUR GREAT EMPIRE!

THIS DAY REMINDS US THAT TOGETHER, WE ARE STRONG. TOGETHER, WE CAN ACHIEVE GREATNESS.
THIS DAY REMINDS US THAT WE AZZAZIANS BOW TO NO ONE! FOR ON THIS VERY DAY, KINGDOMS UNITED WITH A SINGULAR PURPOSE...
...DESTROY THE THEN MIGHTY SONGHAY EMPIRE!

MY BROTHERS AND SISTERS, YESTERDAY I RECEIVED A SIMILAR THREAT TO THE ONE KING SUNNI ALI OF SONGHAY HIMSELF GAVE US.
SO I ASK YOU-- SHOULD I, AS YOUR QUEEN, YIELD TO SUCH BLATANT DISRESPECT?!
NOOOO!
NEVER!
AZZAZ BOWS TO NO ONE!
ALLOW ME TO INTRODUCE MY SPECIAL GUEST...
THE MING DYNASTY WOULD REDUCE YOUR QUEEN TO A LOWLY ASSASSIN...
...DOING THEIR BIDDING IN TIME FOR THEM TO MAKE THEIR WAY DOWN HERE TO TORMENT AND CONQUER US.
JUST AS THEY DID OUR BROTHERS AND SISTERS TO THE EAST...

THE ONLY REASON I AM NOT SENDING YOUR SMUG FACE BACK IN PIECES IS BECAUSE I NEED YOU TO DELIVER A MESSAGE TO YOUR GENERAL...
AZZAZ WILL BOW TO NO ONE.
I THOUGHT YOU SAID IT WAS DONE. MY QUEEN THIS IS A MISTAKE!
LIKE I SAID ABDUL--I DID WHAT WAS BEST FOR AZZAZ.

CHAPTER FOUR

Art by Godwin Akpan

The Nupe Province

The Nupe Province, located to the South of the city of Azzaz, is bordered by the Oyo, Benin, and Nri Kingdoms to the South of the empire. Its capital, the City of Confluence (also called the City of Three Rivers), is the center of trade for all merchants, towns, kingdoms, and empires in West Africa. Chief Jimada currently governs the Nupe Province.

The fictional Nupe Province was inspired by the real-life Nupe people, an ethnic group located in both Central and Northern parts of Nigeria (Niger, Kwara, and Kogi). In *Malika: Warrior Queen*, Nupe Province's fictional City of Confluence, the City of Three Rivers, is inspired by Lokoja, a city located in the Kogi State of Nigeria where the two rivers, Niger and Benue, form a confluence.

MING CAMP, 700 KM SOUTHEAST OF AZZAZ
I CAN'T SEEM TO HEAR YOU. YOU SAID YOU HAD A MESSAGE?
GOOD. YOU ARE HERE.
GRRRR...
IS THAT... IS THAT THE EMPEROR'S ENVOY?
YES... WE HAVE HAD A... DISAGREEMENT. NOW, IF YOU DON'T WANT TO JOIN HIM, I SUGGEST YOU SPEAK.

YES, GENERAL. QUEEN MALIKA... SHE REFUSED.
WAR IT IS, THEN.
ON THEIR OWN LANDS? IS THAT WISE?
THE DRAGON STONES ARE THE MOST POWERFUL RELICS THE WORLD HAS EVER KNOWN. POSSESSING THEM WOULD, THEREFORE, MAKE ME THE MOST POWERFUL BEING THE WORLD HAS EVER KNOWN. TO GET TO THEM, WE MUST GET TO THE WINDMAKER.
TO GET TO *THE WINDMAKER,* WE MUST DESTROY MALIKA. ONLY THEN CAN I BUILD MY OWN DYNASTY.

MALIKA, YOU HAVE DOOMED US ALL! WAR WITH MING IS A RECKLESS AND FOOLISH MOVE!
YOU WOULD HAVE YOUR QUEEN TURN INTO A PETTY ASSASSIN? SPILL THE BLOOD OF AN INNOCENT KING?
AN ALLY? JUST SO WE CAN COWER BEHIND OUR WALLS?
YES! IF IT SAVES OUR PEOPLE!
I KNEW YOU WERE A COWARD, DOGBARI, BUT I HAD NO IDEA YOUR TIMIDITY WAS THIS SEVERE.
MY QUEEN, HE IS NOT ALONE ON THIS MATTER. MANY ON THIS COUNCIL FEEL THE SAME.
THE ALLIANCE WITH ATALA WAS A MISTAKE FROM THE VERY BEGINNING. YOU HAVE BECOME RECKLESS AND IRRESPONSIBLE!
HOW DARE YOU?!
IT IS OKAY. THE COUNCIL OF FIVE WAS FORMED SO EACH PROVINCE COULD HAVE A SAY IN MATTERS OF THE EMPIRE.
AND I AGREE, I HAVE MADE SOME INDEPENDENT DECISIONS IN THE PAST.

THANK YOU, ABDUL. I VALUE YOUR OPINIONS-- EVEN WHEN THEY ARE NOT ALIGNED WITH MINE. WE SHALL TALK STRATEGY TOMORROW.
YES, MY QUEEN.
PERMIT ME TO SAY ONE THING...
OF COURSE.
REMEMBER, LOVE MAKES YOU WEAK. IT WILL EXPOSE YOU BOTH.
YOU LOVED MY MOTHER AND SHE LOVED YOU. YOU BOTH TRIED TO KEEP IT A SECRET, BUT I ALWAYS KNEW. WAS THAT WEAKNESS AS WELL?
YOUR MOTHER IS DEAD... I THINK THAT ANSWERS YOUR QUESTION.

CITY OF CONFLUENCE, NUPE PROVINCE.
INCREDIBLE... IT IS EVEN MORE BEAUTIFUL THAN YOU DESCRIBED IT...
THE CITY OF THREE RIVERS AND THE CENTER OF ALL TRADE.
THE GREAT WEST RIVER FLOWS ALL THE WAY TO LAKE FON, ALLOWING TRADE WITH THE AKAN REGION AND THE GOLD COAST.
THE GREAT EAST RIVER FLOWS THROUGH MOUNTAINS AND PAST THE MANDARA PROVINCE. IT ALLOWS TRADE IN THE FAR EAST AND NORTHEAST REGIONS.
FINALLY, THE NRI RIVER ALLOWS TRADE WITH OUR ALLIES IN THE OYO KINGDOM, THE BENIN KINGDOM, AND THE NRI KINGDOM TO THE SOUTH...
BUT ENOUGH ABOUT ECONOMICS. WE ARE HERE FOR SOMETHING MUCH MORE INTERESTING...
...AND IT IS JUST BEYOND THOSE MOUNTAINS.

THIS PLACE IS REMARKABLE.
YES IT IS... I COME HERE WHENEVER I NEED TO FLEE FROM THE BURDEN OF RULE.
THIS IS WHERE YOU HID DRAGON'S DESTINY?
YES. BUT THAT IS NOT WHY WE ARE HERE.
OF COURSE. I KNOW YOU HAVE A PLAN. YOU ARE CERTAINLY NOT AS *RECKLESS* AS YOUR COUNCIL THINKS.
NOT "AS" RECKLESS?
YOU KNOW WHAT I MEAN.
DID YOU POSITION YOUR MEN AS WE DISCUSSED?
YES. NORTH OF THE *MAMBILA* MOUNTAINS--ABOUT A DAY'S JOURNEY FROM HERE. BUT WHY THERE?
YOU WILL FIND OUT IN TIME. BUT FIRST, I NEED TO SHOW YOU SOMETHING. IT IS A BIT OF A TREK.
SO IN THE MEANTIME, TELL ME MORE ABOUT YOUR *MYSTERY* WEAPONS.
ATALIAN MYTHOLOGY IS... COMPLICATED.
IT IS A LONG WALK...

THOUSANDS OF YEARS AGO, IN THE TIME OF DRAGONS, THERE WAS A MAN NAMED *ATALA*. THE FIRST DRAGON RIDER.

"HE WAS ABLE TO ACCESS THE POWERS OF THE FIVE DRAGONS.
"*GANJU*, THE FIRE DRAGON, *OKUN*, THE FROST DRAGON, *GANSO*, THE SHOCK DRAGON, *MOJA*, THE WATER DRAGON, AND THE SOURCE OF MY POWERS, *YAO*, THE WIND DRAGON.

"ATALA ALONG WITH HIS TWO SONS, *USEH* AND *ORIS*, MIGRATED TO OUR LANDS FROM THE OYO KINGDOM.
"THE FIRST OF MY PEOPLE CALLED THEM *THE DIVINE ONES*.
"ORIS WON MANY BATTLES, ALWAYS PLEASING HIS FATHER, BUT USEH CONSTANTLY TOOK SHORTCUTS.
"ATALA EVENTUALLY GRANTED ORIS DRAGON'S DESTINY, MAKING HIM HIS HEIR.
"FORGED FROM THE ESSENCE AND ELEMENTS OF EACH DRAGON, THE SWORD IS ABLE TO EMIT PURE ENERGY.
"IT IS THE MOST *POWERFUL* WEAPON EVER CRAFTED.

"EVENTUALLY, USEH BECAME JEALOUS. HIS HEART WAS SO FILLED WITH HATRED THAT HE WAS ABLE TO USE IT TO CRAFT A WEAPON OF RIVAL POWER, DRAGON'S DOOM.

"IN HIS RAGE, USEH KILLED HIS FATHER...

"SEVERAL WARS BROKE OUT AS BROTHER FOUGHT BROTHER. THEY CALLED THEM, THE *DRAGON WARS*.

"AFTER YEARS OF WAR, ORIS DEFEATED USEH."

SEEING HOW THE POWER OF THE DRAGONS CORRUPTED PEOPLE AND DESTROYED HIS FAMILY, ORIS TRANSFERRED THEIR ABILITIES INTO WHAT MY ANCESTORS CALLED THE STONES OF ORIS.
AFTER HIS DEATH, THEY SWORE A SACRED OATH TO PROTECT AND CONCEAL BOTH DRAGON'S DESTINY AND DRAGON'S DOOM. AS FOR THE STONES, NO ONE KNEW WHERE ORIS HID THEM.
UNTIL CHENG CAME LOOKING.
CHENG CAME UNDER THE GUISE OF A PEACEFUL PARTNER IN TRADE, BUT OUR ELDERS WERE NAIVE. HE GOT A HOLD OF DRAGON'S DOOM BUT COULD NEVER ACTIVATE ITS POWERS.
WHY NOT?
DRAGON'S DOOM IS ACTIVATED BY PURE RAGE, AND ITS POWER IS ONLY LIMITED BY HOW MUCH OF THAT ITS WIELDER POSSESSES. AS MUCH OF A DEGENERATE AS CHENG IS, HE IS MOTIVATED BY SOMETHING ELSE.
AND DRAGON'S DESTINY--WHAT IS THE SECRET TO ITS POWER?
TRUE COURAGE...FROM THE PERFECT WARRIOR. BUT ITS POWERS WILL ONLY COME TO LIFE IF DRAGON'S DOOM IS ACTIVATED.
YOU WERE NOT JOKING WHEN YOU SAID THIS WAS COMPLICATED.

IT WAS ORIS'S WAY OF PREVENTING FUTURE CHAOS. AND WHY I BROUGHT DRAGON'S DESTINY TO YOU. CHENG CANNOT HAVE BOTH SWORDS. THAT COULD CHANGE EVERYTHING.
EVERYTHING CHANGED WHEN YOU FOUND THE WIND STONE.
YES. WITH MY POWERS, I WAS ABLE TO UNITE MY PEOPLE AND DRIVE CHENG AND HIS ARMY AWAY FROM ATALA.
IT IS EASY TO UNITE YOUR PEOPLE WHEN YOU ARE A DEMIGOD.
WHOOSH
WHOOSH
WHOOSH
IT TOOK MORE THAN POWERS...JUST LIKE IT WILL TAKE MORE THAN BRUTE FORCE TO SUBDUE YOUR COUNCIL.
MY DEAR HUSBAND, HOW LONG WILL YOU PERSIST ON THIS MATTER?
MALIKA, IT IS EASY FOR THE MASSES TO FOLLOW A GREAT LEADER. BUT IT TAKES A GREAT PERSON TO RALLY OTHER LEADERS BEHIND THEM.
YOU REALLY NEED TO BEGIN TO JOURNAL YOUR WORDS OF WISDOM.
IN THE MEANTIME, HOWEVER...
...WE ARE HERE.

MAGNIFICENT...
THIS IS THE FIRST HALF OF THE PLAN.
YOU AZZAZIANS SURELY KNOW YOUR WAY AROUND IRON.
EXTRA PROTECTION WITHOUT SACRIFICING SPEED. I CAN HAVE IT FITTED FOR YOUR RAVENS...
AS LIGHT AS THESE ARE, THEY WILL STILL AFFECT OUR MOVEMENTS. WE NEED TO BE ABLE TO--
MOVE LIKE THE WIND. I KNOW, MY LOVE. WISE WORDS FROM YOUR SHAOLIN MASTER.
I OWE THAT MAN MY LIFE. ***MASTER YU*** AND THE OTHER MONKS FOUGHT WITH US AGAINST CHENG AND PAID THE ULTIMATE PRICE.
HE TRULY MEANT A LOT TO YOU...
HE DID...
...SO, WHAT IS THE OTHER HALF OF THE PLAN?
YOUR POWERS.
MALIKA, WE SPOKE ABOUT THIS. CHENG WILL BE EXPECTING A DIRECT ATTACK.
I NEVER SAID ANYTHING ABOUT A DIRECT ATTACK.

GENERAL, YOUR HORSE IS READY.
THE AZZAZIAN PEASANTS HAVE SEEN IT FIT TO JOIN FORCES WITH THE ATALIANS. AS A MAN FULL OF MERCY, I GAVE THEIR QUEEN A CHANCE TO REDEEM HERSELF.
NOT ONLY DID SHE REFUSE, SHE ALSO DISRESPECTED YOUR EMPEROR. I DO NOT KNOW ABOUT YOU MEN, BUT AS HIS MAJESTY'S LOYAL SERVANT, I WILL NOT TOLERATE SUCH IMPUDENCE!
SO ON THIS DAY, OUR TASK IS SIMPLE. WE WIPE THE AZZAZIANS FROM THE FACE OF THIS EARTH. THEIR WOMEN! THEIR CHILDREN! THEIR ARMIES AND THEIR LEADERS!
AND WHEN WE ARE DONE, ALL THAT IS LEFT OF THEIR EMPIRE WILL BE ASHES! ARE YOU WITH ME?!
YAHHH!!

THANK YOU ALL FOR COMING UNDER SUCH SHORT NOTICE.
WHY ARE WE HERE, DOGBARI?
YOU KNOW WHY. MALIKA NEEDS TO BE STOPPED.
THIS IS *TREASON!* I WILL NOT BE A PART OF THIS.
YOU ALREADY ARE, HAZAR.
WHAT?!
WOULD YOU LIKE THE QUEEN TO BE ALERTED ABOUT YOUR PRESENCE HERE?
YOU WOULD NOT DARE. WE WOULD ALL BE EXECUTED.
IF WE DO NOTHING, WE ARE ALL DEAD ANYWAY. AND FOR THIS TO WORK, WE NEED THE FIVE TO BE IN AGREEMENT. FOR HOW LONG WILL YOU TOLERATE A TYRANT?
WE HAVE BECOME MERE FIGUREHEADS. NO ONE RULER SHOULD BE ABOVE THE COUNCIL. WHEN SHE DECLARED ALL SLAVES TO BE FREE MEN, WE LET THAT BE.
AFTER THE ATALIAN INTERFERENCE, WE SAID NOTHING! NOW WAR WITH MING? THAT NEEDS TO BE CORRECTED.
WHAT DO YOU HAVE PLANNED?
THE SAVIORS OF AZZAZ.
THE REBELS?
TRUST ME... THEY HAVE BECOME A LOT MORE THAN REBELS. WITH THEM AND HOPEFULLY A NEW ALLY, WE WILL ALL FINALLY HAVE OUR ***INDEPENDENCE***.

NRI KINGDOM,
OUTSKIRTS.
GREETINGS...

WHO ARE YOU?
MY NAME IS CHIDI. THIS IS MY LAND. WE ARE JUST A SMALL VILLAGE-- MOSTLY FARMERS FROM THE NRI KINGDOM TO THE WEST. YOUR ARMY IS FREE TO COME AND GO AS YOU PLEASE.
DO YOU STAND WITH THE AZZAZIANS?
NO, WE DO NOT. WE HAVE NO ALLEGIANCE TO ANY OF THE KINGDOMS AROUND THESE PARTS. WE REMAIN NEUTRAL AND INSTEAD ONLY TRADE WITH EACH FROM TIME TO TIME.
YOU SAY YOU ARE NOT FOR THEM, BUT YET YOU TRADE WITH THEM?
YES. I BELIEVE YOU CAN HAVE ONE WITHOUT THE OTHER.

VERY WELL. WE WILL BE ON OUR WAY, THEN.
THANK YOU, GENERAL. SAFE TRAVELS.
ZHANG...
BURN THEM.
YES, GENERAL?
THE WOMEN AND CHILDREN?
BURN THEM ALL.

MOMENTS LATER.

GREAT EAST RIVER, MANDARA PROVINCE.
WHEN I WAS YOUNG, MY MOTHER SENT ME OFF TO ACQUIRE KNOWLEDGE AT SANKORE IN TIMBUKTU. AMONGST MANY SUBJECTS, THE ONE THING I LOVED TO STUDY THE MOST WAS WAR.
I RESEARCHED THE GREATEST OF OUR ANCESTORS--KING MENES, KHUFU, AND KALYDOSOS. I ALSO STUDIED QUEEN NEFERTITI AND KANDAKE.
I IDOLIZED THEM ALL.. ONE OF THE MANY THINGS THEY HAD IN COMMON WAS THEIR ABILITY TO WIN BATTLES DESPITE THE ODDS STACKED AGAINST THEM.
SO IS THIS THE OTHER HALF OF THE PLAN?
THE RIVER...
CHENG HAS TWO WEAKNESSES--OVERCONFIDENCE AND IMPATIENCE. AFTER MY THEATRICS WITH ZHANG, HE WILL BE FURIOUS. KNOWING THAT HIS ARMY OUTNUMBERS OURS 5-1, HE WILL NOT HESITATE TO TRY AND WIPE US OUT.
HOW ARE YOU SO SURE HE WILL USE THIS ROUTE?

THE RIVER IS EASIEST TO CROSS AT THIS POINT.
SO WE USE CHENG'S WEAKNESSES AS OUR STRENGTHS?
EXPLOIT HIS WEAKNESSES, YES. BUT THOSE ARE NOT NECESSARILY THE SOURCE OF OUR STRENGTH...
WHAT IS THEN?
...WHY ME OF COURSE.
SIR, A REPORT!
SPEAK.
GENERAL CHENG'S ARMY APPROACHES. THEY WILL BE HERE IN THREE DAYS. HE HAS ALSO RECRUITED *MERCENARIES* FROM THE EAST.
ZANDE WARRIORS... THAT COMPLICATES THINGS.
ZANDE WARRIORS?

SOME OF THE MOST FEROCIOUS FIGHTERS IN THE EAST.
WE STICK TO THE PLAN.
MY QUEEN, THERE IS ONE MORE THING...
THE VILLAGERS AT THE BORDER... CHENG...HE BURNED THEM ALL...
WHAT?! THOSE PEOPLE WERE NO THREAT!
THIS IS WHAT CHENG DOES. HE IS TRYING TO INTIMIDATE US.
THEIR BLOOD IS ON YOUR HANDS AS WELL. THIS WOULD NOT BE HAPPENING IF--
ABDUL, ENOUGH! KOBA, INFILTRATE CHENG'S CAMP. IT IS TIME WE GATHERED MORE INFORMATION. IF CHENG WANTS RUTHLESS, I WILL GIVE HIM RUTHLESS.

HOW COULD YOU BETRAY ME?!
NADIA, YOU GAVE ME NO CHOICE...
NADIA! NO!!!
HOLD ON! PLEASE! JUST HOLD ON!
NADIA!!!

MALIKA, ARE YOU--
MALIKA, IT IS ALL RIGHT. IT IS ME...
BASS... DID I--
NO... I AM ALL RIGHT.
MALIKA, WHAT TROUBLES YOU?
NOTHING, MY LOVE, JUST A NORMAL DREAM.

YOU WAKE UP IN A COLD SWEAT, ALMOST STABBING YOUR SECRET HUSBAND, AND THIS SOUNDS NORMAL TO YOU?
BASS...
VERY WELL. GO BACK TO SLEEP, THEN.
...THIS IS ALL NEW TERRITORY FOR ME...MY ENTIRE LIFE, ALL I HAVE KNOWN IS WAR. EVEN WHEN I DID NOT WANT TO, I WAS FORCED TO FIGHT.
I HAVE ACHIEVED THINGS MY MOTHER AND FATHER COULD NOT. AND IT IS ALL BECAUSE I NEVER SHOW WEAKNESS.
IT IS ALL RIGHT TO BE STRONG. BUT LOVING SOMEONE... TRUSTING THEM AND BEING VULNERABLE WITH THEM IS NOT WEAKNESS. IT IS TRUE STRENGTH.
YOU ARE A POET NOW? CURSE THE MONKS THAT TAUGHT YOU TO BE THIS NOBLE.
I AM SERIOUS, MALIKA.

THE DREAM...IT WAS ABOUT NADIA. I HAVE BEEN DREAMING ABOUT HER MORE LATELY.
YOU STILL BLAME YOURSELF FOR HER DEATH? THERE WAS NOTHING YOU COULD DO.
I JUST...
YOU MISS HER. IT IS ALL RIGHT TO.
I JUST WISH SHE WAS HERE. WHEN SHE DIED, IT FELT LIKE SOMEONE RIPPED HALF OF MY SOUL AWAY.
THE LOVE YOU TWO HAD FOR EACH OTHER IS ETERNAL. NO ONE CAN EVER TAKE THAT AWAY.
I HAVE NOT CRIED IN YEARS. ABDUL WAS RIGHT-- YOU ARE MAKING ME SOFT.
IT IS ALL RIGHT TO BE SOFT WITH YOUR HUSBAND. LET CHENG HAVE THE IRON FIST.
TRUST ME...HE WILL.

CHAPTER FIVE

Art by Godwin Akpan

The Mandara Province

The Mandara Province is located to the East of the city of Azzaz. The towering Manbila and Mandara Mountains, combined with the rough terrain at the border, provide perfect deterrents to any would-be attackers from the East. Chief Nchare currently governs the Mandara Province.

Mandara Province details in *Malika: Warrior Queen* were inspired by Africa's Mandara Mountains. They are a volcanic range that runs along the Northern part of the Cameroon-Nigeria border.

QUEEN MALIKA, THE GREAT UNIFIER. IT IS AN HONOR TO FINALLY MEET YOU.
GENERAL CHENG. IF YOU TURN YOUR MEN AROUND IMMEDIATELY AND LEAVE, I WILL FORGIVE YOUR TRESPASSING.
THERE IS NO NEED FOR YOUR MEN TO DIE TODAY.
I AM AFRAID I CANNOT DO THAT. YOU SEE, YOU HAVE SET A BAD EXAMPLE FOR THE REST OF THE KINGDOMS ON THIS CONTINENT.
DISRESPECT TO THE EMPEROR CANNOT GO UNPUNISHED...
BROTHER, YOUR QUARREL WAS WITH MY UNCLE. THERE IS NO NEED FOR US TO SPILL EACH OTHER'S BLOOD TODAY.
YOU WILL PAY FOR THE CRIMES OF BAKWA THE BUTCHER.
SO BE IT.
WINDMAKER! YOU LET A WOMAN FIGHT YOUR BATTLES NOW? I WILL HAVE YOUR HEAD BEFORE THIS DAY IS OVER.
AND USE YOUR CORPSE TO TRACK THE REST OF WHAT YOUR PEOPLE HID FROM ME.
IF I WERE YOU, I WOULD PRAY WE DO NOT MEET IN BATTLE TODAY.

AZZAZIANS... TODAY WE FACE AN ENEMY MIGHTIER THAN ANY WE HAVE EVER SEEN BEFORE--AN ENEMY WHO WISHES TO CONQUER US. FEAR IS A LOGICAL RESPONSE, AND I CANNOT PRETEND THAT I DO NOT SEE IT IN SOME OF YOUR EYES.
TODAY WE MAY LOSE. TONIGHT WE MAY PERISH. BUT I WOULD RATHER DIE A THOUSAND DEATHS, IN A THOUSAND LIFETIMES, THAN BECOME A SLAVE ON MY OWN LANDS!
WE ARE AZZAZIANS AND THE BLOOD OF GREAT WARRIORS FLOWS THROUGH OUR VEINS! ALL I ASK FROM YOU TODAY IS THAT YOU FIGHT FOR THE MAN NEXT TO YOU. FIGHT FOR YOUR BROTHERS, YOUR SISTERS, YOUR WIVES, AND YOUR CHILDREN BACK HOME, WHOSE SPIRITS YOU CARRY INSIDE YOU.
LET THEM INSPIRE YOU! AND WHATEVER FEARS YOU FEEL INSIDE, MAKE YOUR ENEMY FEEL A THOUSANDFOLD!
FOR IF WE ARE TO DIE TODAY, WE WILL DIE DEFENDING OUR FREEDOM!
IS EVERYTHING READY?
YES...
FOR AZZAZ! FOR FREEDOM!

FOOL! WHAT DOES SHE THINK SHE'S DOING? SHE CAN'T POSSIBLY HOPE TO ATTACK UPHILL FROM THE RIVERBANK?
A RATHER PECULIAR GAMBIT.
PECULIAR? I THINK NOT. SHE IS DESPERATE AND CLUELESS.
PERHAPS SHE--
MOVE THE MEN INTO POSITION AT THE BANK AND PREPARE COUNTERMEASURES. MAKE SURE THEY REMAIN IN LOOSE FORMATION.
AND KEEP THE ARCHERS HERE. WE CANNOT MAKE IT EASY FOR THE WINDMAKER TO SIMPLY BLOW US AWAY.
DESTROY THEM!!!

CLANG
WHOOSH
THUD
ARGH!
RGHHH!!

WHOOOSH
OH NO...
ARGH!
MALIKA!

THIS IS THE GREAT WARRIOR QUEEN EVERYONE SPEAKS SO HIGHLY OF? SO DISAPPOINTING.
THERE ARE TOO MANY OF THEM!
NGKK.
FALL BACK! RETREAT!

IF SHE THINKS I'M GOING TO LET HER RETREAT, SHE IS MORE FOOLISH THAN I THOUGHT.
ATTACK. FULL SALVO. SEND THE REST OF THE MEN.
POMPUMMMMM
MOVE! HURRY!
BENGU, NOW!
PONPOMPUMMMMMM

TWOOM

WHOOSH
RUN!!!

KING BASS!
I AM ALL RIGHT...
MY KING, YOU CANNOT FIGHT IN THIS CONDITION. YOU NEED TO REST.
I KNOW... MOVE THE REST OF THE MEN INTO POSITION.

NOW THE BATTLE IS EVEN.

WHEEEEWN

GENERAL, WHAT SHOULD WE DO?
GENERAL!
SEN...SEND... SEND THE REST OF THE MEN DOWN TO STOP HER ADVANCE!
ARCHERS! MOVE INTO POSITION!

ADVANCE!
ARCHERS! TAKE AIM!
DISMOUNT! RAISE SHIELDS!
FIRE!

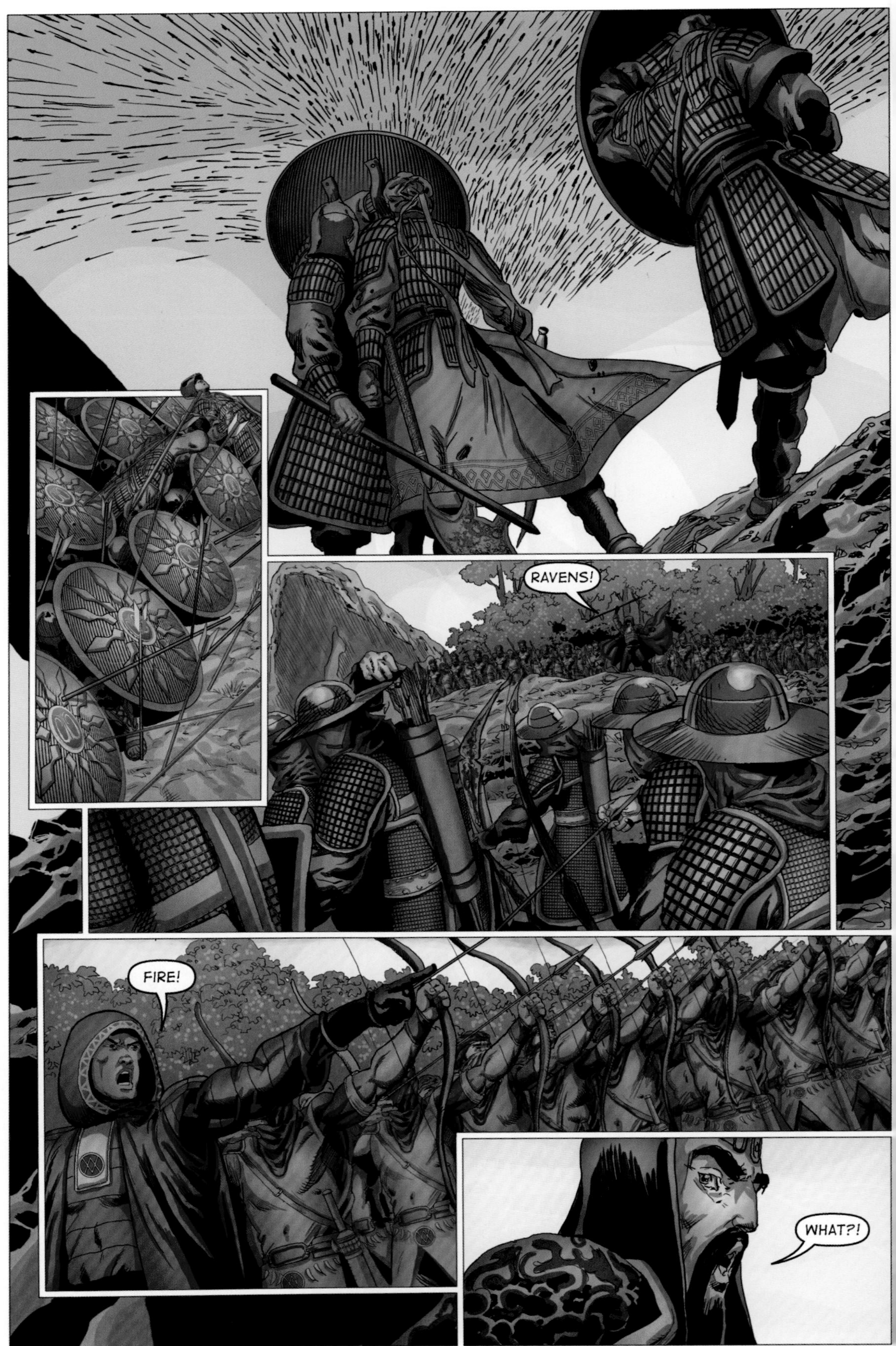
RAVENS!
FIRE!
WHAT?!

ATTACK!
ATTACK THEIR RIGHT FLANK!

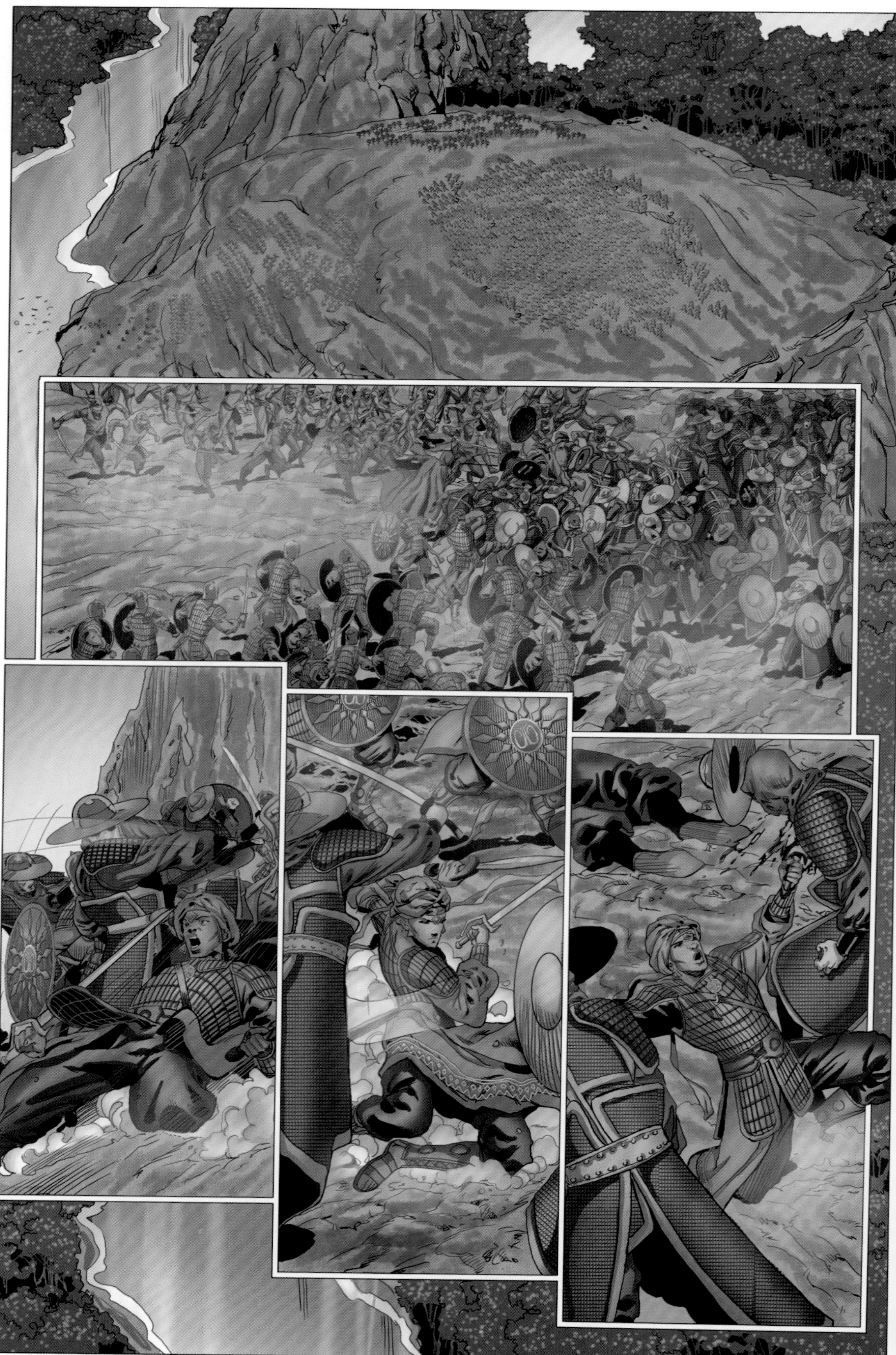

SHUSHHH
SWOOMMM

THUD
RAVENS! HEAD TOWARDS MALIKA'S POSTION!

WEAKLING!

KRACKAAA
COWARDS!

BASS, YOU WERE SUPPOSED TO REMAIN IN POSITION TO RECOVER.

DID YOU REALLY THINK I WOULD?
NO...NOW, LET US END THIS.

I'M GOING AFTER CHENG!

GENERAL, WE HAVE LOST HALF OUR MEN. WE HAVE TO RETREAT!
GENERAL!
ARGHHH!

TAKE THIS,
YOU SPINELESS
COWARD.

FLACK
GENERAL!
GENERAL! WE MUST RETREAT NOW!

FALL BACK! RETREAT!
SHOULD WE FOLLOW?
NO.
I AGREE. HE HAS TOO MUCH OF A HEAD START, AND THEY COULD HAVE SET UP AN *AMBUSH* IN THE FOREST.
BESIDES... I THINK HE GOT THE MESSAGE...

CHAPTER SIX

Art by Godwin Akpan

The Kano Province

The Kano Province, located to the North of the Azzazian empire, is famous for its nomadic cattle raisers. The Azzazian empire depends on the Kano Province for its supply of livestock. Chief Ramfa currently governs this province.

Malika: Warrior Queen's Kano Province was inspired by the Kingdom of Kano, located in what is currently Northern Nigeria. The Kingom of Kano's existence dates back to 1000 AD.

REST WELL, MY BROTHERS...
YOUR MEN FOUGHT BRAVELY.
AS DID YOURS.
JUST AS THE GREAT KING KALYDOSOS DID CENTURIES AGO, YOU HAVE USED YOUR ENEMY'S ARROGANCE AGAINST THEM. YOUR STRATEGY WON US A GREAT VICTORY TODAY.
YET SOMETHING STILL *TROUBLES* YOU.
IT VEXES ME HOW WELL YOU KNOW ME...
I WOULD NOT BE MUCH OF A HUSBAND IF I DID NOT. NOW, TELL ME WHY SUCH A BEAUTIFUL FACE IS MIRED BY WORRY?

ALL THIS... I AM STARTING TO BELIE--
I AM STARTING TO THINK THAT MAYBE THERE'S MORE TO RULE THAN THIS...
WHAT IF THERE IS...WHAT IF YOU COULD INSP--
MY QUEEN...
ABDUL...YOU FOUGHT WELL TODAY.
IT IS ALWAYS AN HONOR FIGHTING BY YOUR SIDE, MALIKA.
YOU AND I NEED TO RETURN TO AZZAZ TO SETTLE POLITICAL MATTERS. WE WILL LEAVE THE BULK OF THE MEN HERE SHOULD CHENG TRY TO ATTACK AGAIN. GENERAL KADAR WILL BE IN CHARGE.
BASS, YOU SHOULD SEND SOME OF YOUR MEN BACK TO ATALA AS WELL. JUST TO BE SAFE.
AGREED. BUT THE RED KNIGHTS WILL REMAIN WITH ME, SHOULD WE NEED THEM.
QUEEN MALIKA. WE WERE ABLE TO CAPTURE THESE COWARDS FLEEING THE BATTLEFIELD.
WE SHOULD MAKE EXAMPLES OF THEM. LET US SEND THEIR HEADS TO CHENG.

PLEASE...HAVE MERCY...
TRANSPORT THESE MEN TO THE PRISONS IN AZAAZ. THEY ARE TO REMAIN THERE UNTIL I CAN DECIDE HOW BEST TO REFORM THEM. TILL THEN, NO HARM IS TO BE DONE TO THEM.
IT TAKES A GREAT PERSON RIGHT?

MY QUEEN! I URGE YOU! THESE MONSTERS MUST PAY FOR THEIR CRIMES WITH THEIR LIVES!
I SEE NO MONSTERS HERE, ABDUL--JUST TERRIFIED MEN FOLLOWING ORDERS.
MALIKA, THIS IS AN ATROCITY. THIS IS WEAKNESS! THE FIVE HAVE SPIES EVERYWHERE.
THEY WILL EXPLOIT THIS. YOU CANNOT AFFORD TO FIGHT A WAR BOTH ON THE OUTSIDE AND FROM WITHIN. THESE ARE NOT OUR WAYS!
THEN MAYBE OUR WAYS NEED TO CHANGE, ABDUL... I WILL SEE YOU AT HOME.
KING BASS... A WORD?
THIS VICTORY WOULD NOT HAVE BEEN POSSIBLE WITHOUT YOU.
WE ALL HAD OUR PARTS TO PLAY, ABDUL. I MERELY DID MINE.

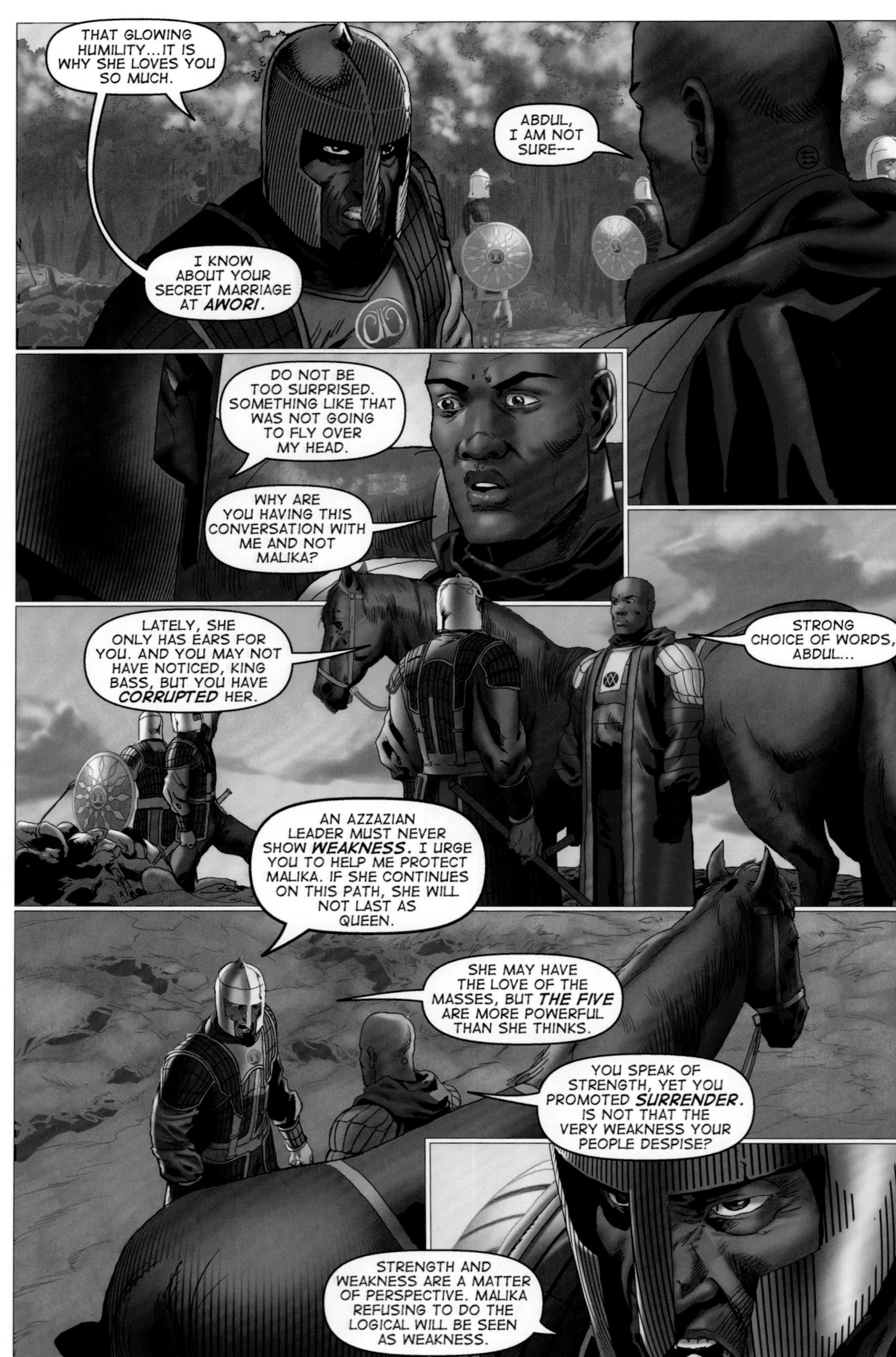
THAT GLOWING HUMILITY...IT IS WHY SHE LOVES YOU SO MUCH.
ABDUL, I AM NOT SURE--
I KNOW ABOUT YOUR SECRET MARRIAGE AT AWORI.
DO NOT BE TOO SURPRISED. SOMETHING LIKE THAT WAS NOT GOING TO FLY OVER MY HEAD.
WHY ARE YOU HAVING THIS CONVERSATION WITH ME AND NOT MALIKA?
LATELY, SHE ONLY HAS EARS FOR YOU. AND YOU MAY NOT HAVE NOTICED, KING BASS, BUT YOU HAVE CORRUPTED HER.
STRONG CHOICE OF WORDS, ABDUL...
AN AZZAZIAN LEADER MUST NEVER SHOW WEAKNESS. I URGE YOU TO HELP ME PROTECT MALIKA. IF SHE CONTINUES ON THIS PATH, SHE WILL NOT LAST AS QUEEN.
SHE MAY HAVE THE LOVE OF THE MASSES, BUT THE FIVE ARE MORE POWERFUL THAN SHE THINKS.
YOU SPEAK OF STRENGTH, YET YOU PROMOTED SURRENDER. IS NOT THAT THE VERY WEAKNESS YOUR PEOPLE DESPISE?
STRENGTH AND WEAKNESS ARE A MATTER OF PERSPECTIVE. MALIKA REFUSING TO DO THE LOGICAL WILL BE SEEN AS WEAKNESS.

ABDUL, CHENG IS ON THE RUN.
CHENG IS BUT A COG IN THE DESTRUCTIVE WAR MACHINE KNOWN AS THE MING DYNASTY.
WHAT EXACTLY WOULD YOU HAVE ME DO?
HAVE HER SEND A MESSAGE TO THEIR EMPEROR. USING THE PRISONERS AS GOOD FAITH, WE CAN STRIKE A DEAL WHILE WE STILL HAVE THE UPPER HAND.
IT IS THE ONLY WAY WE CAN END THE WARS ON THE OUTSIDE AND WITHIN.
MALIKA IS MORE THAN CAPABLE OF MAKING HER OWN DECISION AND IS WISE ENOUGH TO KNOW WHEN TO EVOLVE. QUITE FRANKLY, SHE IS THE GREATEST LEADER I HAVE EVER KNOWN.
AND YOU NEED TO START TREATING HER AS SUCH INSTEAD OF ALWAYS PERCEIVING HER AS YOUR STUDENT.
IT IS AN IMPOSSIBLE TASK. BUT STILL, I URGE YOU TO TRY...
...PERHAPS YOU SHOULD HAVE JUST SURRENDERED YOURSELF BEFORE ALL THIS BEGAN. NOW YOU HAVE PUT YOURSELF, MALIKA, AND YOUR UNBORN CHILD IN GRAVE DANGER.

GET OUT!
BESTED BY A SIMPLETON!
GENERAL CHENG. WE...WE HAVE... WE HAVE RECEIVED WORD FROM THE EMPEROR.
AND WHAT WORD WOULD THAT BE?!
AH...

SPEAK!
YES, GENERAL!
"BY THE ORDER OF THE EMPEROR, GENERAL CHENG IS TO RETURN TO BEIJING IMMEDIATELY. REFUSAL TO DO SO WILL BE TREATED AS TREASON."
GENERAL, IT IS VERY UNWISE TO DISOBEY THE EMPEROR. AND EVEN IF YOU DECIDE TO, THE MEN ARE WEARY, TIRED, AND HOMESICK. ONLY HALF OUR FORCES REMAIN, WE SHOULD--
SILENCE! I DO NOT RECALL ASKING FOR YOUR COUNSEL.
I HAVE MALIKA RIGHT WHERE I WANT HER...
SO BE IT...
...SEND THEM IN.

THE "SAVIOR OF AZZAZ"... SEEMS I SHOULD HAVE TRUSTED YOU EARLIER. WELL, NOW YOU HAVE WHAT YOU REQUESTED...
LET US SEE WHAT YOU CAN DO WITH DRAGON'S DOOM.

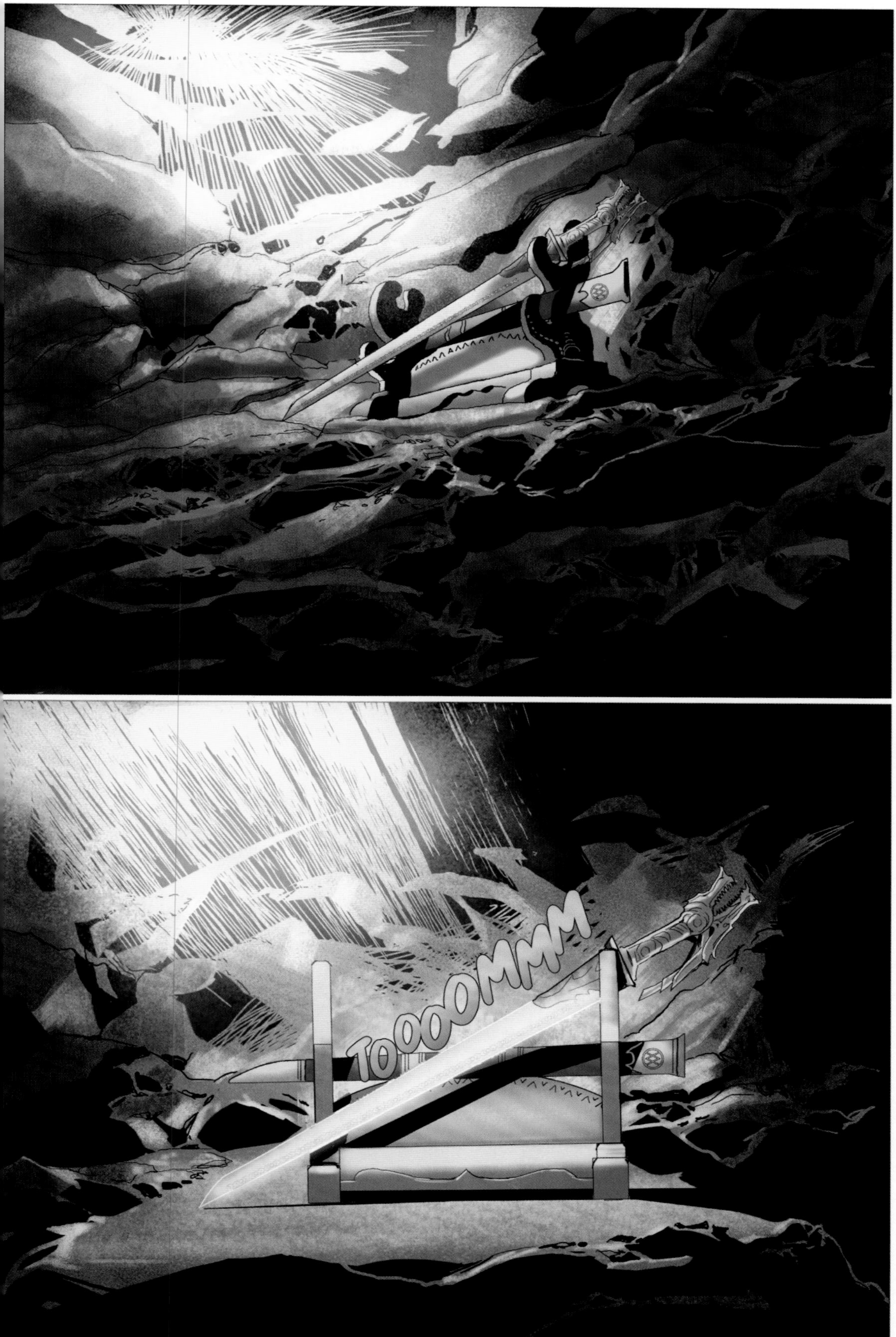

TOOOOMMM

THIS NECKLACE IS BEAUTIFUL.
NOTHING IS AS BEAUTIFUL AS YOU, MY LOVE.

FIRST A GIFT AND NOW FLATTERY? AND NOT JUST ANY GIFT, BUT ONE MADE OUT OF YOUR PRECIOUS ROCK. LET US SEE WHERE YOU ARE GOING WITH THIS...

ABDUL USED TO MAKE ME AND NADIA JEWELRY LIKE THIS WHEN WE WERE YOUNGER... BEFORE HE TURNED INTO A GRUMPY OLD MAN.
HE SPOKE TO ME AFTER YOU LEFT.

I WAS WONDERING HOW LONG IT WOULD TAKE BEFORE HE GAVE YOU A LECTURE.

MALIKA... HE TOLD ME THERE WAS A *CHILD*...IS IT TRUE?
YES...
MY LOVE!
YOU ARE NOT ANGRY?
OF COURSE I AM. I AM JUST TOO HAPPY TO SHOW IT! MALIKA, WHY KEEP IT FROM ME?
BECAUSE I KNOW YOU, BASS. YOU WOULD HAVE ***SURRENDERED*** YOURSELF RATHER THAN SEE ME FIGHT.

OF COURSE I WOULD HAVE. AND I MORE THAN LIKELY WILL DO THAT NOW. ABDUL WAS RIGHT. I SHOU--
BASS STOP.
I NEED YOU...WE... NEED YOU. NOW MORE THAN EVER.
MALIKA, CHENG WILL NOT STOP. HOW ELSE CAN I PROTECT YOU TWO?
LET HIM COME. WE WILL KEEP FIGHTING.
MALIKA, I CANNOT RISK--
BASS, FROM THE MOMENT YOU CAME INTO MY LIFE, I BEGAN TO SEE THINGS DIFFERENTLY.
BUT IT DOES NOT CHANGE THE FACT THAT WHEN IT COMES TO WAR, ***NO ONE*** HAS EVER DEFEATED ME.
I NEED YOU TO TRUST ME ON THIS, JUST LIKE I HAVE LEARNED TO TRUST YOU ON OTHER MATTERS.

CHENG IS NOT YOUR ONLY ENEMY.
I AM WELL AWARE OF THE ENEMIES WITHIN MY WALLS. TRUST ME, I FEAR NONE OF THEM.
NOW PLEASE, CAN WE DISCUSS THIS LATER AND PREPARE FOR THE CELEBRATION TONIGHT?
WHAT ARE WE CELEBRATING?
THE FIVE HAVE SPENT A DECENT AMOUNT OF TIME SINCE OUR TRIUMPH PUTTING TOGETHER A VICTORY FEAST...DURING THE CELEBRATION, I WILL FINALLY ANNOUNCE OUR MARRIAGE.
I LOVE--
MY QUEEN, A WORD.
GO ON.

THERE HAVE BEEN SOME STRANGE REPORTS ABOUT A PERSON WITH...MYSTICAL POWERS...ATTACKING A VILLAGE NEARBY.
MYSTICAL POWERS?
YES, MY QUEEN.
VERY WELL...THANK YOU.
IF THIS IS WHAT I THINK IT IS, THEN WE NEED TO SECURE--
BASS, IT IS PROBABLY NOTHING. I GET REPORTS LIKE THESE ALL THE TIME. BUT IF IT PLEASES YOU WE CAN HEAD TO THE ARMORY AFTER THE CELEBRATION. I NEED YOU TONIGHT. BESIDES, YOU ARE STILL TOO WEAK TO USE YOUR POWERS.
I DO NOT NEED THEM...BUT ALL RIGHT. I WILL SEND THE RED KNIGHTS TO PROTECT DRAGON'S DESTINY, JUST IN CASE.

BAM
BAM
BAM
I AM GLAD YOU DECIDED TO JOIN US...
ABDUL... SHALL WE BEGIN? THE COUNCIL AWAITS...

CHAPTER SEVEN

Art by Mohammed Agbadi

THE YOUNEEK YOUNIVERSE

Raised in the Royal Palace in the city of Azzaz, once she inherits control of her empire Malika deals with rebels within as well as intruders from outside of Azzaz—before she sets out on other extraordinary adventures beyond its borders with magical sword Dragon's Destiny. Malika's story in *Malika: Warrior Queen* Volume 1 takes place in the same universe as the *Iyanu: Child of Wonder*, *E.X.O.: The Legend of Wale Williams*, and *WindMaker* graphic novels—the YouNeek YouNiverse.

YEARS AGO.
GRAND MASTER, WE FOUND THE BODY.
ALIVE OR DEAD?
ALIVE... BARELY.
GOOD. COMMENCE PREPARATIONS.
GRAND MASTER, I MEAN NO DISRESPECT, BUT SHOULD WE BE USING THIS MUCH DARK MAGIC ON THE SUBJECT?
WE CAN BARELY CONJURE ENOUGH TO STAY ALIVE OFF THE ISLAND. WE SHOULD---
HOW MANY YEARS HAVE I ENSURED THE SURVIVAL OF *THE ORDER*?
FOR MILLENNIA, GRAND MASTER.
AND YET YOU STILL QUESTION ME?
GRAND MASTER, I SIMPLY--
KNOW YOUR PLACE, APPRENTICE. ELSE I WILL PUT YOU THERE IN WAYS YOUR DISRESPECTFUL SOUL WILL DREAD.
YES, GRAND MASTER.
IT BEGINS, MY LORD.

MOMENTS LATER.
AARGGHHHHH!!!!!
AS YOU PREDICTED, GRAND MASTER, SHE IS A PERFECT MATCH.
THE HATE BURNS INSIDE HER. BUT HER INJURIES ARE TOO SEVERE. SHE WILL NOT SURVIVE THE DAY.
WHO ARE YOU PEOPLE? WHERE AM I? WHY AM I--
ARGGH!!!
SAVE YOUR ENERGY, CHILD. YOU ARE SEVERELY INJURED.
IF NOTHING IS DONE, YOU WILL PERISH BEFORE THE SUN SETS.
WHO... ARE YOU?

WE ARE THE ORDER OF THE OLON JIN. AND YOUR LAST HOPE FOR SURVIVAL.
YOU PEOPLE... YOU PEOPLE ACTUALLY EXIST?
WE ARE HERE, ARE WE NOT?
AND HOW DO YOU PLAN ON SAVING ME?
DARK MAGIC.
NO! NEVER! LET ME GO IMMEDIATELY!
I WILL NEVER YIELD TO SUCH...
TO SU...
SHE IS UNCONSCIOUS. SHALL WE PROCE--
GRAND MASTER, WE SPOTTED A BATTALION OF AZZAZIAN SOLDIERS NOT TOO FAR FROM HERE.
THEY SEARCH FOR HER. NO ONE CAN KNOW SHE IS HERE.
VERY WELL. I WILL RALLY THE REST OF THE--
NO. I WILL TAKE CARE OF THIS MYSELF. KEEP HER ALIVE, WHATEVER IT TAKES. FOR THIS TO WORK, SHE MUST ACCEPT OUR TERMS WILLINGLY.
YES, GRAND MASTER.

CAPTAIN! I HAVE NEWS!
SPEAK.
I FOUND A TRAIL. I THINK WE MAY HAVE A LOCATION.
GOOD.
MEN! PREPARE TO MARCH!

MOMENTS LATER.
HALT!
CITIZEN, I AM GOING TO HAVE TO ASK YOU TO MOVE IMMEDIATELY.
I AM NO CITIZEN.
STILL...YOU ARE OBSTRUCTING THE ARMY OF THE GREAT QUEEN JOHARA.
MOVE. OR I WILL HAVE TO ARREST YOU.
YOU CAN TRY.
ENOUGH OF THIS! ARREST HER!

WITCH! KILL HER!
HMPFFF!
KRRKIK
WAAM
WHAT?!
POOF

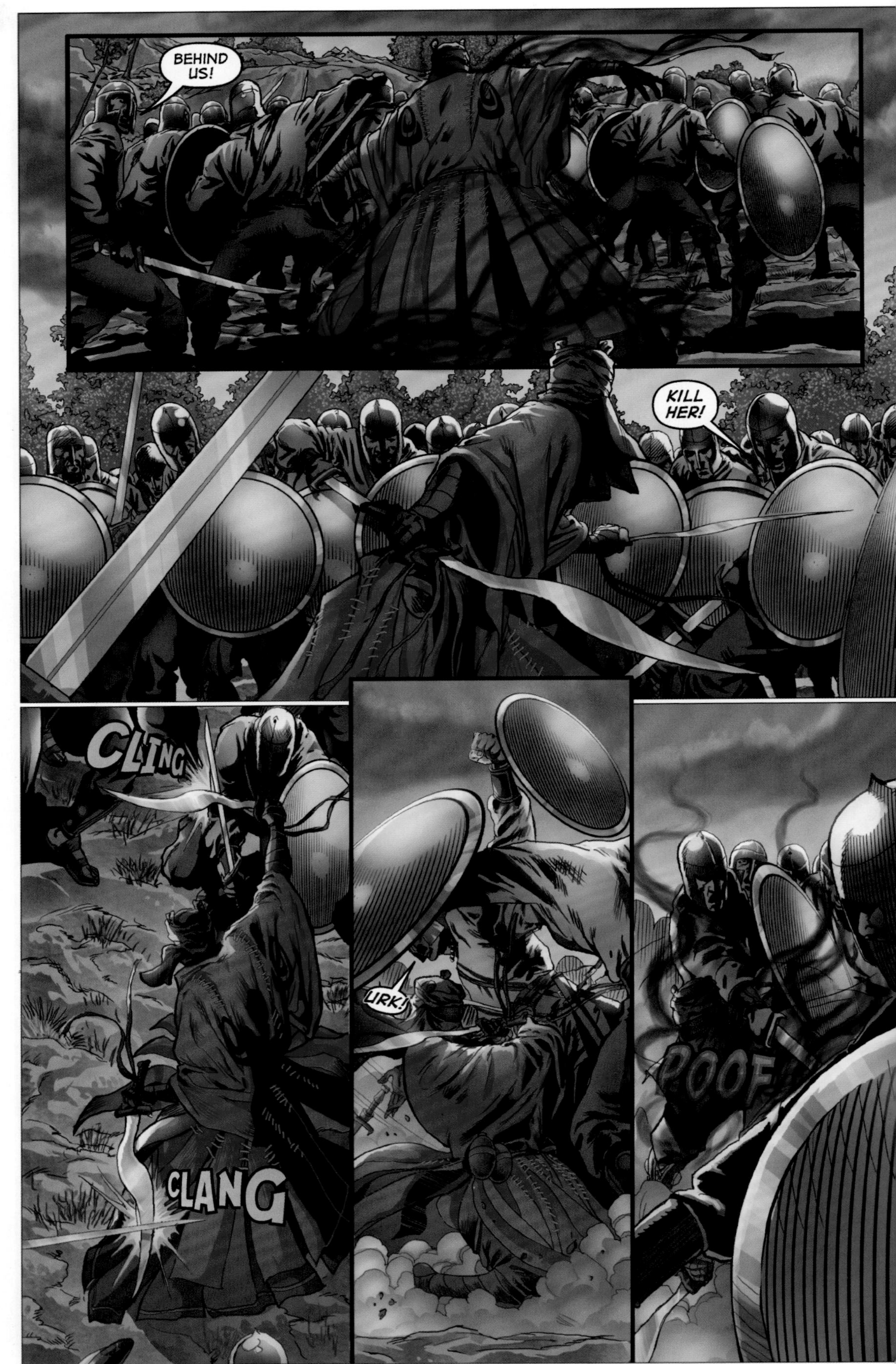
BEHIND US!
KILL HER!
CLING
CLANG
URK!
POOF

OOF!
ARR!!
POOF
SWACK
SSLITTCH
AARRGH!!
POOF
URK!

UARGH!
WAM
POOF
POOF
POOF
SSLITTCH
POO
ARRGH!!

NHMMPPFF...
NNRR...
DEMON... WHAT ARE YOU?
PATIENCE.
ARCKGHH...
YOUR KIND WILL SOON FIND OUT.
POOF

Present day.

MALIKA!
MALIKA!!
ALL HAIL QUEEN MALIKA!
ALL HAIL QUEEN MALIKA!!
CONGRATULATIONS ON YOUR VICTORY, MY QUEEN. THEY WILL SING YOUR PRAISES FOR ETERNITY.
MALIKA! MALIKA!!
MY BROTHERS AND SISTERS, TODAY WE GATHER TO CELEBRATE, ONCE AGAIN, THE BRAVERY OF OUR GREAT QUEEN, MALIKA!
SHE, ALONG WITH KING BASS AND THE BRAVE RED RAVEN ARMY, HAVE DRIVEN THE MIGHTY MING DYNASTY OFF OUR LANDS!

WHERE IS ABDUL? IT IS ODD THAT HE IS ABSENT.
DO NOT WORRY ABOUT ABDUL. HE IS WHERE HE NEEDS TO BE.
"AS A TEENAGER, AGAINST ALL ODDS, SHE DEFEATED SUNNI ALI THE GREAT AND THE SONGHAY EMPIRE.
"AND NOW, OUR QUEEN HAS DONE IT AGAIN. AS GENERAL CHENG COWERS IN FEAR, WE CELEBRATE VICTORY!"
BUT NOT JUST ANY VICTORY. AS OF HER LAST BATTLE, QUEEN MALIKA HAS BESTED HER FOES ONE HUNDRED TIMES WITHOUT DEFEAT!
MALIKA. YOUR MEN, DID THEY ROTATE SHI--
"CITIZENS OF AZZAZ, I GIVE YOU QUEEN MALIKA, THE GREAT UNIFIER."
MALIKA!!
BASS... STOP WORRYING SO MUCH.

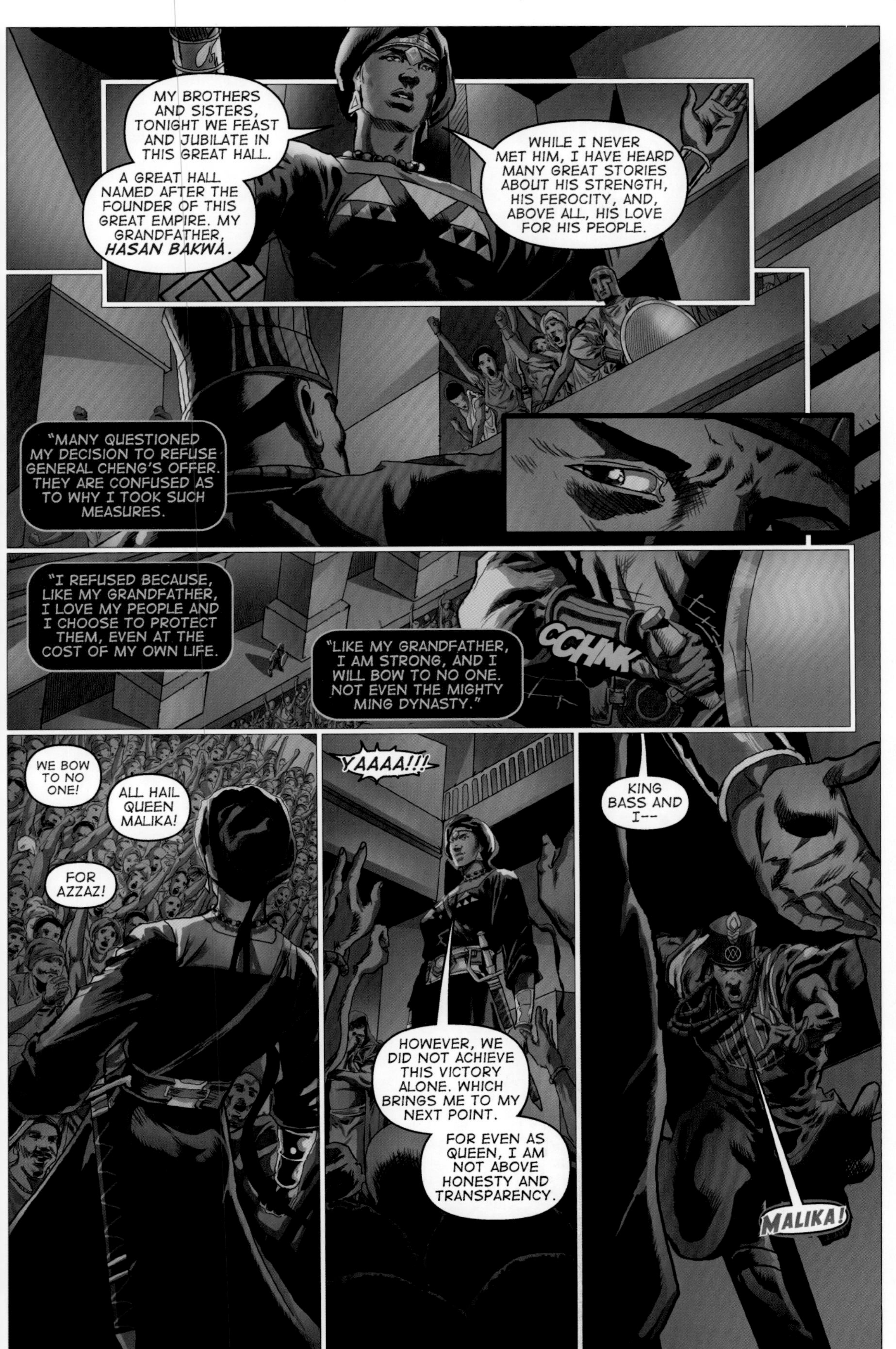
MY BROTHERS AND SISTERS, TONIGHT WE FEAST AND JUBILATE IN THIS GREAT HALL.
A GREAT HALL NAMED AFTER THE FOUNDER OF THIS GREAT EMPIRE. MY GRANDFATHER, HASAN BAKWA.
WHILE I NEVER MET HIM, I HAVE HEARD MANY GREAT STORIES ABOUT HIS STRENGTH, HIS FEROCITY, AND, ABOVE ALL, HIS LOVE FOR HIS PEOPLE.
"MANY QUESTIONED MY DECISION TO REFUSE GENERAL CHENG'S OFFER. THEY ARE CONFUSED AS TO WHY I TOOK SUCH MEASURES.
"I REFUSED BECAUSE, LIKE MY GRANDFATHER, I LOVE MY PEOPLE AND I CHOOSE TO PROTECT THEM, EVEN AT THE COST OF MY OWN LIFE.
CCHNK
"LIKE MY GRANDFATHER, I AM STRONG, AND I WILL BOW TO NO ONE. NOT EVEN THE MIGHTY MING DYNASTY."
WE BOW TO NO ONE!
ALL HAIL QUEEN MALIKA!
FOR AZZAZ!
YAAAA!!!
HOWEVER, WE DID NOT ACHIEVE THIS VICTORY ALONE. WHICH BRINGS ME TO MY NEXT POINT.
FOR EVEN AS QUEEN, I AM NOT ABOVE HONESTY AND TRANSPARENCY.
KING BASS AND I--
MALIKA!

TWIP
TWIP
AARRGH!!
MALIKA! NO!
TWIP
TWIP
TWIP
WHOOSH
THUD
MALI---
KAAAH
THUD
THUD
THUD
BASS!!!

BASS!!!
MA... MALIKA...
SAVE YOUR STRENGTH, MY LOVE. SHHH... QUIET. KEEP YOUR EYES ON ME.
POISON... ARROWS... I DO NOT HAVE LONG.
NO, NO, NO. YOU CANNOT. YOU WILL NOT LEAVE ME! CAN YOU HEAR ME?! WE HAVE A FAMILY NOW. OUR CHILD NEEDS YOU. I NEED YOU. BASS!
MY WIFE... MY LOVE...IN ALL THE EARTH, NONE COMPARE TO YOU. THE JOY YOU HAVE BROUGHT ME CANNOT BE QUANTIFIED.

BASS, PLEASE. STAY WITH ME. PLEASE.
I WILL ALWAYS BE WITH YOU. BUT... YOUR PURPOSE... IS MUCH BIGGER THAN AZZAZ.
I CAN SEE IT NOW. REMEMBER... LOVE... MERCY... FORGIVENESS.
I... LOVE... YOU...
BASS... BASS... BASS!!!
BASS...

SLIN
STOP! LOWER YOUR WEAPONS.
WHICH AMONGST YOU MEN IS STUPID ENOUGH TO BETRAY ME?
NOT A *MAN*...

A QUEEN.
NA...NADIA? HOW...HOW CAN...YOU ARE ALIVE?
CLANG

BUT OF COURSE I AM, MY DEAR SISTER.
HOW IS THIS POSSIBLE? I SAW YOU. YOU FELL. AT THAT HEIGHT IT WOULD BE IMPOSSIBLE FOR ANYONE TO--
HOW I SURVIVED IS NOT IMPORTANT. WHAT I WOULD LIKE TO DISCUSS IS HOW YOU HAVE MANAGED TO DESTROY MY KINGDOM.
YOUR KINGDOM?

THE REBELS... IT WAS YOU.
THE SAVIOR OF AZZAZ, IN THE FLESH. SEEMS YOU STILL HAVE MUCH TO LEARN ABOUT YOUR PEOPLE. YET, EVEN THE THINGS YOU DID LEARN, YOU FORGOT!
YOU HAVE BECOME SOFT AND ERRATIC! SPARING PRISONERS, STARTING A WAR YOU CANNOT WIN, AND MY PERSONAL FAVORITE, MARRYING A FOREIGNER.
NADIA, HOW CAN YOU DO THIS?!
URGH!
BECAUSE YOU ARE A POOR EXCUSE FOR A QUEEN.

NOW, WHICH ONE OF YOU FIRED AT MY SISTER?
RRRGH...
IT...IT WAS US. THE WINDMAKER, HE WAS ABOUT TO ATTACK. WE HAD NO CHOICE.

TWOOM
AARRGH!!
YOU WERE TOLD TO WAIT UNTIL I WALKED IN.
DRAGON'S DOOM. NADIA, WHERE DID YOU GET THAT WEAPON?
CHENG, OF COURSE.
NADIA, LISTEN TO ME. THAT WEAPON IS CORRUPTING YOU. YOU NEED TO---
HOW DARE YOU OPEN YOUR MOUTH TO SPEAK OF CORRUPTION? YOU, WHO SELFISHLY ALIENATED YOUR COUNCIL AND PUT A DEATH SENTENCE ON YOUR PEOPLE.

BUT FEAR NOT. I HAVE A PLAN THAT WILL SAVE OUR PEOPLE AND BRING US OUT OF THE MESS YOU PUT US IN. WE WILL RISE TO BE A MORE PROSPEROUS EMPIRE THROUGH OUR NEW ALLIANCE.
AN ALLIANCE WITH THE MING DYNASTY.
WHAT?! NADIA, LISTEN TO YOURSELF!
SILENCE! YOU NO LONGER HAVE ANY AUTHORITY, MALIKA. YOUR REIGN IS OVER. NADIA IS, AND HAS ALWAYS BEEN, OUR RIGHTFUL QUEEN.
DOGBARI, YOU CONSPIRE WITH OUR ENEMIES, DOOM OUR PEOPLE, AND BETRAY ME.
FOR WHAT? AUTONOMY OVER YOUR LANDS?
"AND DO YOU REALLY THINK CHENG WILL HONOR HIS WORD?!"
YOU DOOMED US ALL, MALIKA. YOU LEFT US NO CHOICE.
THERE IS ALWAYS A CHOICE!

THAT WE CAN AGREE ON. SO HERE IS YOURS. THE POISON IS SPREADING TOWARD YOUR HEART. YOU DO NOT HAVE LONG.
SURRENDER TO ME, ***RENOUNCE*** THE CROWN, AND ENSURE A PEACEFUL TRANSITION.
RESIST, AND YOU WILL QUICKLY JOIN YOUR HUSBAND IN THE AFTERLIFE.
YOU ARE NO SISTER OF MINE. THE NADIA I KNOW IS DEAD. I WILL DESTROY THIS IMPOSTER.
ALONG WITH ALL YOU TRAITORS!
KILL HER.

KKRRRRR KKRRRRRR
WHAT?! WHAT IS--
BOOM
POOF
BOOM
POOF
BOOM
BOOM
SWACK
POOF
POOF

MEN! COUGH DO NOT LET HER COUGH ESCAPE! COUGH
TOO LATE. SHE ALREADY HAS.
COUGH COUGH
COUGH COUGH
COUGH COUGH
WELL PLAYED, ABDUL.
THEY ESCAPED!
OH, ARE YOU SURE?
THIS IS NOT THE TIME TO JEST.
NEITHER IS IT THE TIME TO POINT OUT THE OBVIOUS. FIND THEM!
WHY? SHE IS AS GOOD AS DEAD.
THE PEOPLE MUST SEE THAT MY SISTER IS DEFEATED. AND I MADE A PROMISE TO CHENG.
SO, IF YOU FIVE TRULY WANT YOUR *INDEPENDENCE*, YOU WILL STOP THIS MINDLESS DEBATE AND BRING ME BOTH BODIES.
UNDERSTOOD. BLOCK ALL THE EXITS. NO ONE LEAVES THE CITY. PREPARE THE MEN TO SEARCH EVERY CORNER OF THE CITY!

SE... CRET...AR... MORY...

THE SECRET ARMORY? ALL RIGHT. WE SHALL HEAD THERE.

JUST HOLD ON!

CHAPTER EIGHT

The Olon Jin

After committing an unforgivable crime, the Divine Ones cast them out to live in isolation on the Forbidden Island for eternity. With rebellion embedded deep within their souls, the Olon Jin have once again begun to plot a treacherous plan to secure their freedom.

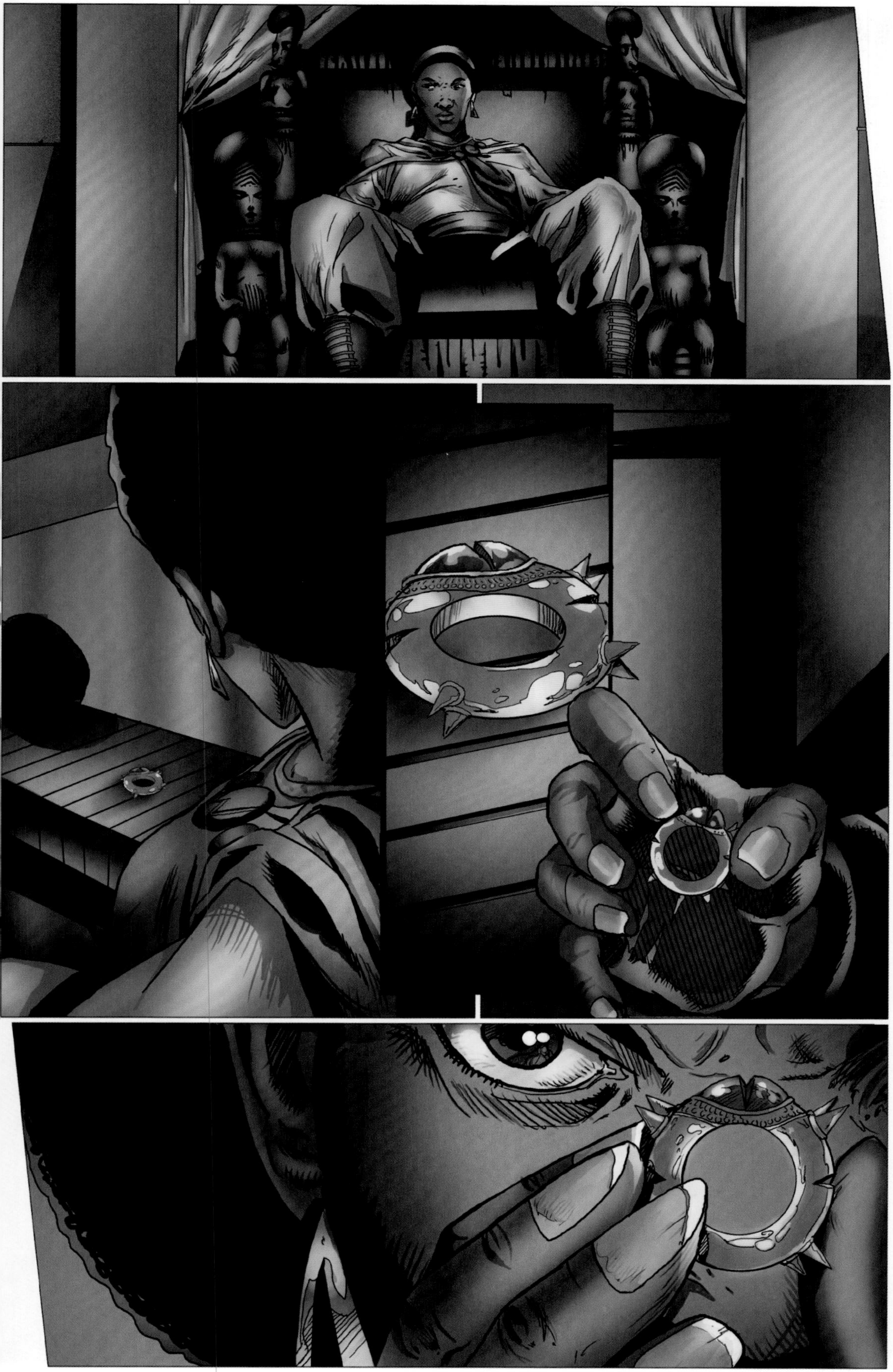

THE OLD PALACE, CITY OF CONFLUENCE.
IN ALL MY YEARS, I HAVE YET TO SEE A MORE BEAUTIFUL VIEW.
I REMEMBER WHEN FATHER WOULD STAND HERE WITH BOTH OF US, TELLING US STORIES OF HIS GREAT BATTLES.
HE WAS A GREAT KING, AND A BETTER FATHER. ONE WHO LOVED HIS CHILDREN DEARLY. UNLIKE OUR QUEEN MOTHER, WHO CLEARLY *FAVORS* YOU.
NADIA...
WHY HAS SHE ASKED US HERE, MALIKA?
NADIA, THERE'S SOMETHING I SHOULD HAVE TOLD YOU.
WHAT?
I HAD TO---
NADIA! WHAT HAVE YOU DONE?!

MOTHER, WHAT IS THE MATTER?
DESPITE MY WARNINGS, YOU STILL WENT AHEAD AND DESTROYED YET ANOTHER VILLAGE?!
MALIKA, HOW COULD YOU BETRAY ME?
NADIA, WHAT CHOICE DID I HAVE? THIS WAS THE FIFTH TIME. HUNDREDS OF INNOCENT PEOPLE... HOW COULD I STAY SILENT?
HOW MANY TIMES MUST I TELL YOU: WE CANNOT SIMPLY KILL PEOPLE TO COERCE LOYALTY. THIS IS NOT THE WAY!
I DID THIS FOR YOU, YET YOU QUESTION MY METHODS? MY PASSION TO SEE YOU THE VICTOR IN THIS CIVIL WAR?!
THIS IS NOT PASSION, THIS IS RAGE. AND I WILL NOT HAVE IT!
NADIA, STOP AT ONCE!
I CANNOT BELIEVE THIS!
STAY HERE.

NADIA!
YOU ARE SO WEAK, MOTHER! WHAT I DO WORKS! ELIMINATING THOSE WHO DO NOT COMPLY HAS BROUGHT US MUCH NEEDED RESPECT!
THEY DO NOT RESPECT YOU, THEY FEAR YOU. AND THAT WILL ONLY LAST UNTIL THEY FEAR SOMEONE ELSE. THERE ARE BETTER WAYS TO GATHER ALLIES.
I HAVE NOT THE TIME FOR YOUR SENTIMENTAL DRIVEL, MOTHER! I WILL CONTINUE TO FOLLOW MY INSTINCTS AND WIN US THIS WAR!
NO, YOU WILL NOT. I HAVE HAD ENOUGH OF YOUR INSOLENCE AND RAGE!
FROM THIS MOMENT YOU ARE STRIPPED OF YOUR BIRTHRIGHT. YOU WILL NO LONGER BE HEIR TO THE THRONE. THAT WILL GO TO YOUR SISTER. IT IS CLEAR YOU WILL NEVER BE FIT TO RULE.
WH... WHAT?!

HOW DARE YOU, MOTHER?! YOU WOULD TAKE AWAY THE ONE THING I HAVE WORKED FOR ALL MY LIFE? BECAUSE OF YOUR LOVE FOR YOUR GOLDEN CHILD?
MY DEAR CHILD, THIS IS ALL MY FAULT. I SHOULD HAVE SEEN IT YEARS AGO. I HAVE FAILED YOU.
DO NOT PATRONIZE ME, MOTHER! THIS IS WHAT YOU HAVE ALWAYS WANTED. TO CROWN YOUR FAVORITE, MALIKA.
YOUR JEALOUSY TOWARD YOUR SISTER IS PART OF THE REASON WE ARE HERE.
WHY DO YOU ALWAYS FEEL YOU HAVE TO PROVE YOU ARE BETTER?
BECAUSE YOU GIVE ME NO ROOM TO BE MYSELF. YOU CONSTANTLY PRAISE HER WHILE YOU *CRITICIZE* ME. AND NOW YOU HAVE TAKEN EVERYTHING AWAY FROM ME. AND FOR THAT YOU WILL *PAY!*

NADIA, PLEASE.
YOU TRAITOR! THIS IS WHAT YOU HAVE ALWAYS WANTED!
NADIA, YOU KNOW IN YOUR HEART THAT IS FALSE. PLEASE STOP THIS MADN--
LET GO OF ME, TRAITOR!
NADIA, CONTROL YOURSELF THIS INSTANT.
NADIA, WATCH OUT!
NADIA! NO!!!
HOLD ON! PLEASE! JUST HOLD ON!

HOLD ON!!!
NADIA...
I HATE YOU.
NO!

CRCKRMM
MY QUEEN.
YOU SEN... YOU SE... *COUGH*
I AM SURPRISED YOU CAN STILL SPEAK OR STAND.
YOU DISPLAYED AN INCREDIBLE LEVEL OF STUPIDITY WHEN YOU ACCEPTED MY SISTER'S *CHALLENGE*.
I ASSURE YOU, MY QUEEN, IT WILL NOT AFFECT MY DUTIES TO YOU.
GOOD. SEND WORD TO GENERAL CHENG. IT IS TIME WE WELCOMED OUR ALLIES TO AZZAZ.
YES, MY QUEEN.

Art by Godwin Akpan

CHAPTER NINE

Malika, Queen of Azzaz

"Writing the books in the *Malika* series has been one of the most exciting times for me as a writer. And one of the main reasons is because, as someone who was born and raised in Lagos, Nigeria, I get to infuse African history directly into the story. Malika's story is inspired by Queen Amina—a Hausa warrior queen who in the 16th century ruled Zazzau, the African kingdom located in the region now known as Zaria, a city located in the north-central part of Nigeria. Queen Nzinga of Ndongo (modern day Angola), who fought bravely against invaders in the 17th Century, was also a huge source of inspiration for the creation of *Malika*."

—Creator Roye Okupe

CITY OF CONFLUENCE, NUPE PROVINCE.
WE MUST ATTACK NOW, ABDUL!
ATTACKING NOW IS COMPLETELY FOOLISH. WE HAVE TO BE PATIENT.
PATIENT? YOUR PEOPLE MURDERED MY KING. IN COLD BLOOD! THERE MUST BE RETRIBUTION! AND WE MUST HAVE IT NOW!
IF WE ATTACK NOW, WE WILL BE DESTROYED. WE SIMPLY DO NOT HAVE THE NUMBERS.
THEN WE WILL DIE AVENGING OUR KING! AND TAKE AS MANY OF THEM AS WE CAN WITH US!
AND WHAT WOULD THAT ACHIEVE? THE MOST ELITE OF THE RED RAVEN ARMY, MASSACRED SENSELESSLY?
WHO WILL PROTECT ATALA? IS THIS WHAT YOUR KING WOULD WANT?

MY KING IS DEAD! AND HIS BLOOD IS ON YOUR HANDS!
ARGGHH!
MNRGH...
MALIKA!
NO!
I AM SORRY.
SLINN!

MY QUEEN, I RETURNED TOO LATE. I HAVE FAILED YOU MISERABLY. MY LIFE IS YOURS TO TAKE.
HOW LONG HAVE I BEEN ASLEEP?
TWO DAYS, MY QUEEN.
TAKE ME TO HIM.
MALIKA, PLEASE. YOU MUST REST. WE NEED TO--
RRGHHH... ABDUL, YOU MAY HAVE SLOWED THE POISON, BUT MY TIME WILL SOON BE UP. TAKE ME TO HIM.
YES, MY QUEEN.

MING CAMP, 700 KM SOUTHEAST OF AZZAZ.
GENER--
YES, GENERAL. HE SAVED YOU.
BUT I NEVER TOLD YOU FROM WHAT.
DID I EVER TELL YOU THE STORY ABOUT HOW I MET OUR FORMER EMPEROR? FATHER OF OUR CURRENT WOULD-BE RULER.
YOU SEE, WHEN I WAS ABOUT YOUR AGE, I LIVED IN THE SLUMS OF BEIJING.
ABANDONED BY MY PARENTS AT BIRTH, I WAS FORCED TO STEAL AND BEG JUST TO SURVIVE.
ONE DAY, AS I STARVED IN THE GUTTERS, I HEARD A LOUD TRUMPET. TO MY AMAZEMENT, IT WAS THE EMPEROR. EVEN MORE SURPRISING WAS THE FACT THAT HE STOPPED RIGHT IN FRONT ME.
I WILL NEVER FORGET THAT DAY, FOR EVEN BACK THEN I SAW THE PRIVILEGE IN THE EYES OF HIS SON. THE SAME PRIVILEGE WE SEE TODAY IN HIS EYES AS SUCCESSOR.

FOR REASONS HE NEVER TOLD ME, THE EMPEROR RESCUED ME THAT DAY FROM MY MISERY, AND LATER GAVE ME ONE TASK. TO PROTECT HIS **HEIR**.
THE **ONLY** THING HE EVER GAVE TO ME FOR YEARS OF LOYAL SERVICE WAS THIS PAINTING, ON HIS DEATHBED. HE SAID, "NEVER FORGET HOW BEAUTIFUL THE EMPIRE IS."
SINCE THEN, I HAVE HAD TO BRIBE, LIE, STEAL, AND KILL MY WAY TO THE TOP. AND NOW THE VERY CHILD I TRAINED AND PROTECTED WISHES TO TAKE AWAY THE EMPIRE I PLAN TO BUILD FOR MYSELF.
GENERAL... **FATHER**, THIS IS ALL WRONG. OUR ENTIRE CAMPAIGN HERE. AND NOW ARE WE TO BECOME REBELS? AND THE MEN, FOR HOW LONG WILL THEY OBEY?
MY MEN WILL FOREVER BE LOYAL TO ME!
BUT THEY ARE ALSO LOYAL TO THE EMPEROR. AS WELL AS THEIR FAMILIES, WHO THEY HAVE NOT SEEN IN MORE THAN A DECADE. HOW LONG BEFORE THEY REVOLT?
THEY KNOW NOT TO DARE! NOW, I SUGGEST YOU GIVE YOUR REPORT AND LEAVE THE POLITICS TO ME, BOY.
FATHER, PLEASE LISTEN TO REASON! I CANNOT IN GOOD JUDGEMENT CONTINUE TO--
REPORT!!!

VERY WELL. MALIKA HAS "FALLEN." QUEEN NADIA HAS SEIZED THE THRONE.
AND THE WINDMAKER?
DEAD. BUT HIS BODY WAS TAKEN. THE AZZAZIANS ARE CURRENTLY TRYING TO RETRIEVE IT.
ALSO, QUEEN NADIA HAS INVITED YOU TO THE ROYAL PALACE. SHE ASSURES YOU THAT BY THE TIME YOU ARRIVE SHE WILL PERSONALLY HAND YOU THE WINDMAKER'S HEAD.
READY THE MEN. WE RIDE FOR AZZAZ IMMEDIATELY.
YES, MY LORD.

BASS, MY LOVE.
I AM SO SORRY.
I KNEW THE FIVE WOULD TRY TO BETRAY ME. BUT I COULD NEVER HAVE ACCOUNTED FOR NADIA. HOW IS SHE STILL ALIVE?
I DO NOT KNOW. BUT YOUR PLAN WORKED. PRETENDING TO BETRAY YOU ALLOWED ME TO LEARN WHAT THE COUNCIL OF FIVE HAD PLANNED. BUT I, TOO, COULD NOT HAVE PREDICTED NADIA WAS ALIVE.
SHE SAW RIGHT THROUGH THE RUSE AND PUT ME IN CHAINS. I WAS FORTUNATE TO ESCAPE, BUT NOT IN TIME TO SAVE KING BASS.

"THEIR PLAN WAS TO SNEAK INTO THE PALACE USING A PATH KNOWN BY FEW."
"THE TUNNELS MY FATHER BUILT DURING THE FIRST SONGHAI WARS."
"YES.
"NADIA HAS BEEN TRAINING THE REBELS FOR QUITE SOME TIME.
"SHE LED A PORTION OF THEM THROUGH THE TUNNELS AND KILLED A NUMBER OF THE GUARDS IN THE PALACE COMPOUND.
"AFTER THAT, SHE HAD HER MEN DISGUISED IN AZZAZIAN ARMOR PROVIDED BY THE FIVE."

THE CELEBRATION... IT WAS A TRAP. BASS TRIED TO WARN ME. THE MEN THAT FIRED WERE REBEL ASSASSINS.
WE NEED TO RETREAT FARTHER SOUTH WHILE WE FIGURE OUT A PLAN. WE HAVE ALLIES IN THE NRI KINGDOM, WITH HEALERS THAT CAN HELP YOU.
RGGHHH. THERE IS NO PLAN, ABDUL.
MALIKA, IF WE DO NOTHING, EVERYTHING YOU WORKED FOR WILL BE DESTROYED. THE EMPIRE CRUMBLED. YOUR PEOPLE KILLED, OR WORSE, ENSLAVED.
WHAT HOPE DO WE HAVE?
WE CANNOT LET THE ATROCITIES COMMITTED BY YOUR SISTER STAND. WE WILL HAVE OUR VENGEANCE WITH OR WITHOUT YOUR HELP.

ARE YOU THIS BLINDED BY REVENGE?! AND WHERE WERE THE RAVENS DURING THE ATTACK?
PROTECTING AN ANCIENT PIECE OF SCRAP METAL.
WE WERE INSTRUCTED BY OUR KING TO PROTECT IT. KING BASS WOULD NOT HAVE SENT US HERE IF--
THE SWORD. THAT IS THE ANSWER.
THE ANSWER TO WHAT?
WHAT WE DO NEXT.

MALIKA, THE LAST TIME YOU WIELDED THAT WEAPON NOTHING HAPPENED. WHAT HAS CHANGED?
EVERYTHING. WHEN I WAS ASLEEP, WHAT I THOUGHT TO BE A *DREAM* WAS ACTUALLY A *TEST*.
A TEST? MALIKA, I DO NOT UNDERSTAND.
"THE DOOM OF DARKNESS...MUST YIELD TO THE LIGHT OF THE PERFECT WARRIOR."

TOOOOOMMMMM
IMPOSSIBLE!

MY QUEEN, AS REQUESTED, THESE ARE THE MEN WHO--
AARGHHHRRRRR!!!
MY QUEEN, ARE YOU ALL RIGHT?
MY QUEEN!
MY QU--
MY EARS ARE PERFECTLY FINE, RAS. I HEARD YOU THE FIRST TIME.

APOLOGIES, MY QUEEN. FOR A MOMENT I THOUGHT--
SPEAK, RAS.
VERY WELL, MY QUEEN.
THESE ARE THE MALIKA LOYALISTS WE CAUGHT LAST NIGHT TRYING TO SNEAK INTO THE PALACE. PRESUMABLY TO ASSASSINATE YOU.
YOU ARE NO QUEEN OF OURS! WE WILL--
SWACK
SILENCE, CRETIN!
ASSASSINATION. IS THAT SO?
YES, MY QUEEN.
UNSHACKLE THEM IMMEDIATELY.
WHAT?!

QUESTION ME AGAIN, AND IT WILL BE YOUR LAST UTTERANCE.
UNDERSTOOD, MY QUEEN.
RETURN THEIR WEAPONS AS WELL.
YOU MEN HAVE COME FOR VENGEANCE, HAVE YOU NOT? TO REMOVE ME FROM MY PLACE AS RIGHTFUL RULER?
WHAT SORT OF RULER MURDERS HER OWN BLOOD FOR THE THRONE?
CLEARLY, YOU KNOW NOTHING ABOUT POLITICS.
BUT THAT IS TO BE EXPECTED, GIVEN THAT YOU ARE A SIMPLE BRUTE. SO I MIGHT AS WELL SPEAK IN THE LANGUAGE YOU UNDERSTAND.
YOU CAME TO AVENGE "YOUR QUEEN"? WELL, HERE IS YOUR CHANCE. STRIKE ME DOWN IF YOU CAN.
TO MAKE IT FAIR, I WILL NOT USE MY WEAPON, AND MY MEN WILL NOT INTERFERE. YOU HAVE MY WORD.

DIE, WITCH!
AARRGH!!
KOOM
OMPHF!

OOF!
SO DISAPPOINTING.
GET THIS FILTH OUT OF MY SIGHT AND EXECUTE THEM BEFORE SUNDOWN.
HOW DID SHE BECOME SO POWERFUL?
RRRGHH...

WHOOM
MALIKA, ARE YOU--
ALL IS WELL, ABDUL.

RED RAVENS. MY BLOOD. MY PEOPLE. THEY HAVE TAKEN YOUR KING.
THEY HAVE TAKEN MY HUSBAND. AND THEY HAVE TAKEN MY KINGDOM. YOU ALL SEEK VENGEANCE, RETRIBUTION... JUSTICE?!
SO DO I. I MAKE YOU THIS PROMISE: SOON YOU WILL RECEIVE ALL THREE.
YAAA!!
YAAA!!
YAAA!!
TODAY YOUR ANCESTORS SAW IT FIT TO GRANT ME THIS POWER. THE POWER OF THE ANCIENT DRAGONS. THIS IS NOT FORTUITY, THIS IS DESTINY!
I ASK YOU, BRAVE PROTECTORS OF ATALA, WILL YOU HELP ME FREE MY PEOPLE AND AVENGE YOUR KING?!
FOR OUR KING!
THEN I SUGGEST YOU PREPARE YOURSELVES. FOR SOON, WE WILL BRING WITH US RECKONING!
YES!!

YOU SEEM... BETTER.
I BELIEVE THIS WEAPON MAY HAVE BOUGHT ME SOME ADDITIONAL TIME.
HOW?
I AM NOT SURE. BUT I CAN FEEL A PRESENCE WITHIN ME. AS IF SOMEONE IS TRYING TO COMMUNICATE.
BUT HOW STRONG DO YOU FEEL?
STRONG ENOUGH TO DEFEAT NADIA. AND DESTROY EVERY SINGLE REBEL, SOLDIER, CIVILIAN, AND ALLY WHO SUPPORTS HER CLAIM. THE STREETS OF AZZAZ WILL BLEED RED.
I DISAGREED A LOT WITH KING BASS. BUT, IN HIS DEATH I HAVE STARTED TO SEE REASON IN HIS WISDOM. YOU MUST KNOW THAT MOST WHO FOLLOW NADIA DO IT OUT OF FEAR OR IGNORANCE.
IGNORANT OR AFRAID, EVERYONE MUST TAKE RESPONSIBILITY FOR THEIR ACTIONS. ALL WILL FEEL MY WRATH.

Art by Godwin Akpan

CHAPTER TEN

Bass Kazaar, King of Atala

Bass Kazaar (AKA the WindMaker) and his kingdom, Atala, are both heavily influenced by Yoruba culture (the Yoruba being one of the three major tribes in Nigeria). While Atala itself is a fictional nation, its history pulls several tidbits from Yoruba lore, one being that the Atalians are direct descendants of Yoruba people who emigrated from Ife, an ancient Yoruba city in Southwestern Nigeria.

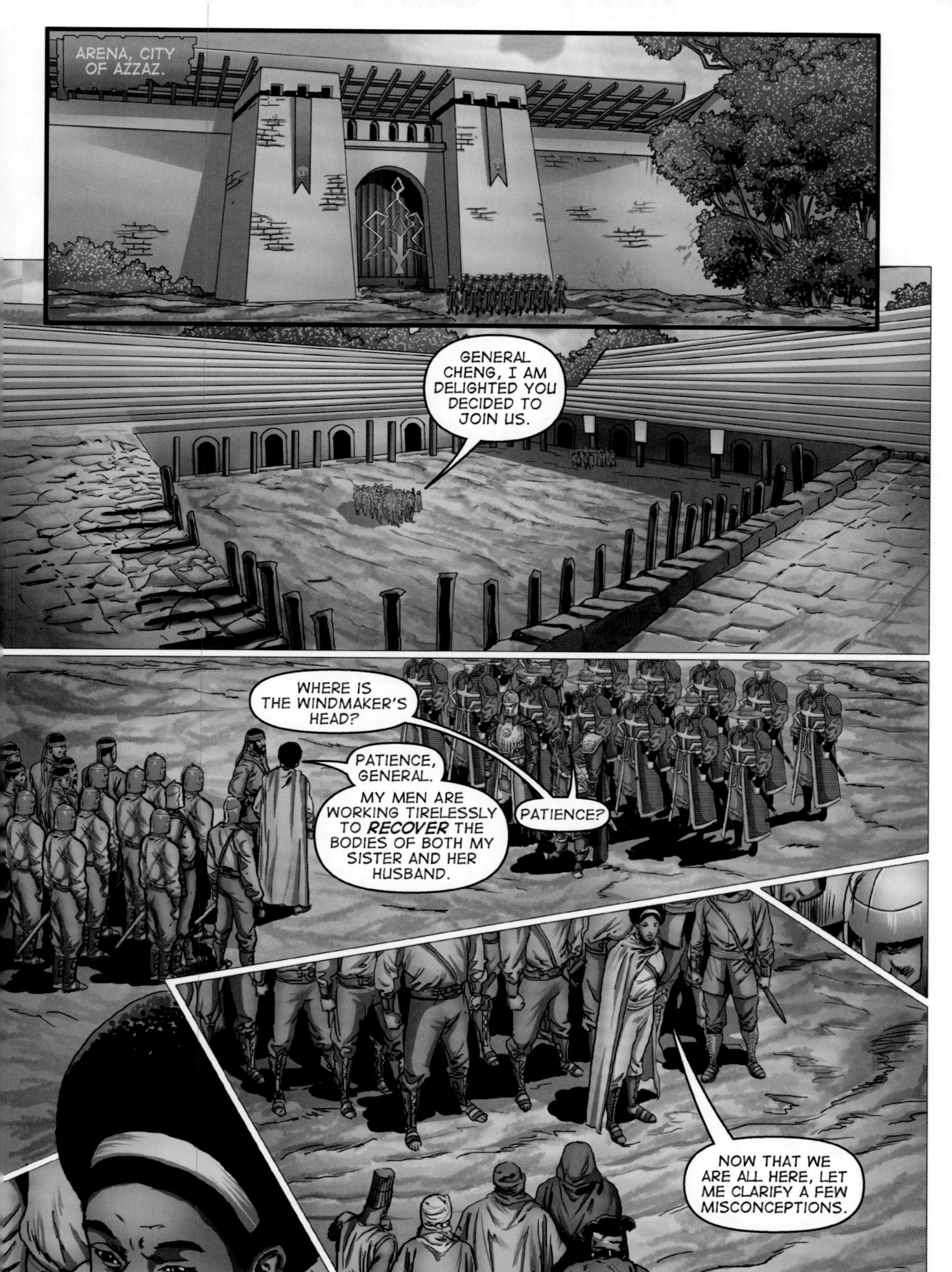
ARENA, CITY OF AZZAZ.
GENERAL CHENG, I AM DELIGHTED YOU DECIDED TO JOIN US.
WHERE IS THE WINDMAKER'S HEAD?
PATIENCE, GENERAL.
MY MEN ARE WORKING TIRELESSLY TO RECOVER THE BODIES OF BOTH MY SISTER AND HER HUSBAND.
PATIENCE?
NOW THAT WE ARE ALL HERE, LET ME CLARIFY A FEW MISCONCEPTIONS.
I DON'T HAVE PATIENCE FOR WEAKNESS.

MARRYING YOUR SON WILL SOLIDIFY OUR ALLIANCE, ALLOW US TO DESTROY THE NEIGHBORING KINGDOMS, AND CONQUER LANDS FROM THE KONGOLESE EMPIRE IN THE EAST TO THE FEUDING MALI AND SONGHAI IN THE WEST.
HOWEVER, DO NOT CONFUSE MY KEENNESS FOR THIS ALLIANCE FOR WEAKNESS.
NEED I REMIND YOU THAT YOU WERE ALREADY LOSING A WAR TO MY SISTER?
THINK ON THAT THE NEXT TIME YOU FEEL I AM ACTING "WEAK."
PLEASE, LET US ALL FOCUS ON THE POSITIVES.
QUEEN NADIA, GENERAL CHENG, ON BEHALF OF THE COUNCIL, THANK YOU FOR RESTORING ORDER TO THE DEBACLE MALIKA INITIATED.
I MUST SAY, IT IS A PLEASURE TO FINALLY BE AMONGST OTHER LIKE-MINDED LEADERS.
"OTHER" LEADERS?

I...WE...PER OUR AGREEMENT, THE EMPIRE WAS TO BE *DISSOLVED*.
WE EACH GET TO INDEPENDENTLY RULE OUR PROVINCES, WHILE YOU RULE THE KINGDOM OF AZZAZ. JUST AS IT WAS BEFORE THE SECOND SONGHAI WAR.
YOUR FOOLISH ASSUMPTION BRINGS ME TO MY NEXT POINT.
FOR HOW LONG WOULD YOUR *AGREEMENT* LAST BEFORE YOU TREACHEROUS SEPARATISTS BETRAY ME?
WHEN WILL YOU IDIOTS LEARN?
DO NOT BE FOOLISH, NADIA! YOU MAY HAVE YOUR REBELS, BUT WITH MALIKA DEAD, THE AZZAZIAN ARMY HAS NO CHOICE BUT TO BE LOYAL TO *THE COUNCIL*. YOU NEED US. NOW, HONOR OUR AGREEMENT!

EIAARRGH!!
EVERYONE IS LOYAL TO FEAR!
FRRTZZZZZ

NOW YOU ARE FREE TO RULE AS YOU PLEASE.
IN THE AFTERLIFE.
THERE IS BUT ONE RULER IN AZZAZ, AND IT IS I. THIS EMPIRE HAS OUTGROWN ITS NEED FOR THE COUNCIL.
IT NO LONGER NEEDS THE RIDICULOUS POLITICS OF YOU LOT REPRESENTING YOUR PROVINCES.
IT IS THAT VERY DIVISION THAT HAS RUINED OUR UNITY, CAUSED YEARS OF CIVIL WARS, AND SPILLED THE BLOOD OF AZZAZIANS.
FATHER, WHY DID WE GIVE HER SUCH POWER IF WE COULD USE IT FOR OURSELVES?
BESIDES, DO NOT BE FOOLED. THAT POWER TAKES MORE THAN IT GIVES.
THERE IS NO LENGTH I WILL NOT GO TO ACHIEVE THIS.
STONES THAT WILL BECOME THE PILLARS OF MY NEW DYNASTY BUILT ON THIS CONTINENT.
WE NEED THE WINDMAKER'S BODY TO TRACK THE REST OF THE DRAGON STONES.
SHE IS TOO UNSTABLE. WHAT IF SHE DECIDES TO KILL US?
BREAK AN ALLIANCE AND KILL A MING GENERAL OUTSIDE THE CONFINES OF WAR? NO MATTER OUR DIFFERENCES, THE EMPEROR WILL BE FORCED TO AVENGE ME.
NADIA WILL THEN HAVE THE WRATH OF THE ENTIRE DYNASTY AT HER DOORSTEP. NO ONE IS THAT FOOLISH.
IN THE AGE OF THE AZZAZIAN AND MING COALITION, WE WILL BECOME THE MOST POWERFUL EMPIRE ON THE CONTINENT.
SO, NOT ONLY ARE WE NOT "LIKE-MINDED," YOU SWINE WERE NEVER EVEN LEADERS.

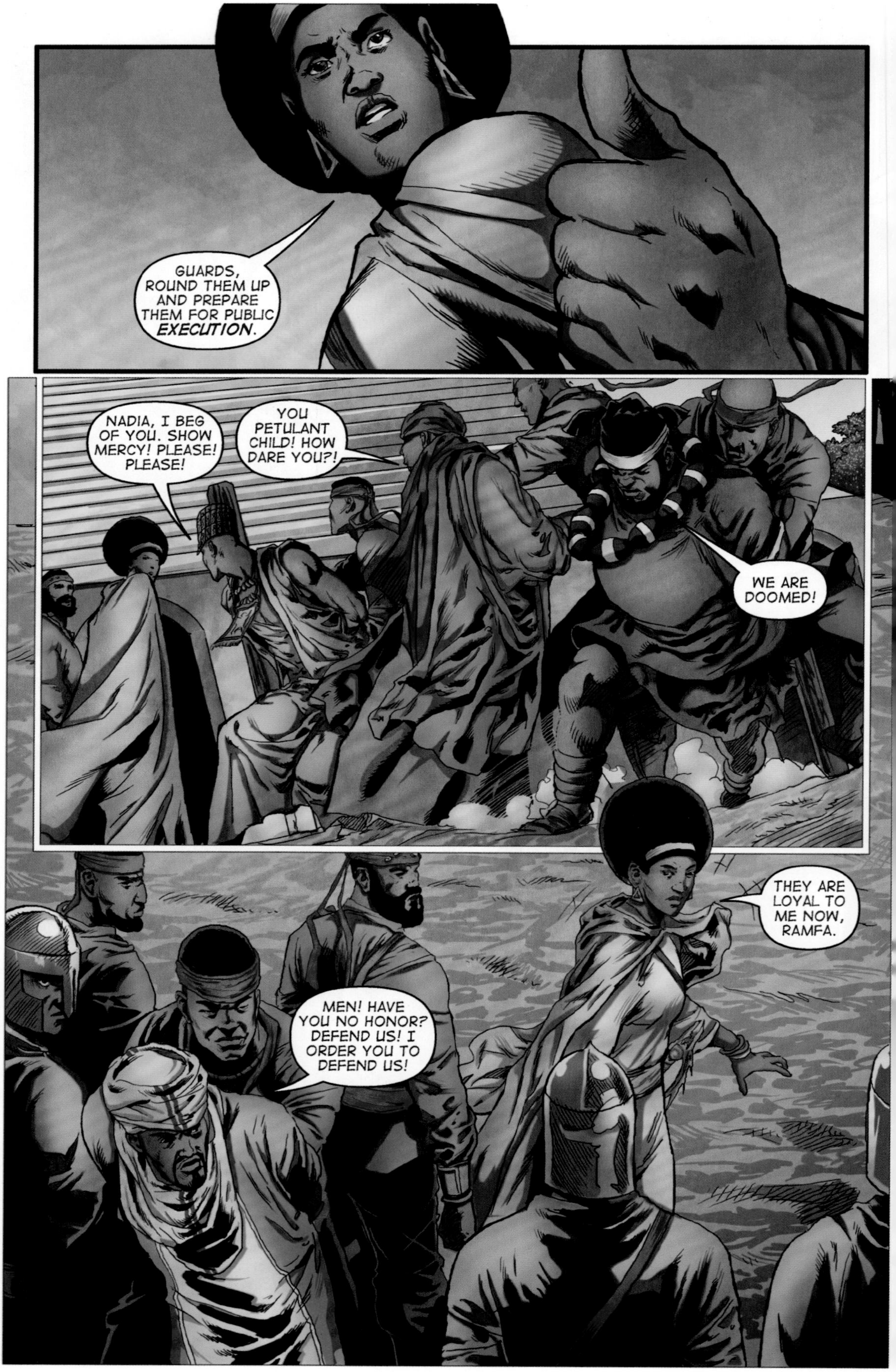

NADIA, I BEG OF YOU. SHOW MERCY! PLEASE! PLEASE!

YOU PETULANT CHILD! HOW DARE YOU?!

WE ARE DOOMED!

THEY ARE LOYAL TO ME NOW, RAMFA.

MEN! HAVE YOU NO HONOR? DEFEND US! I ORDER YOU TO DEFEND US!

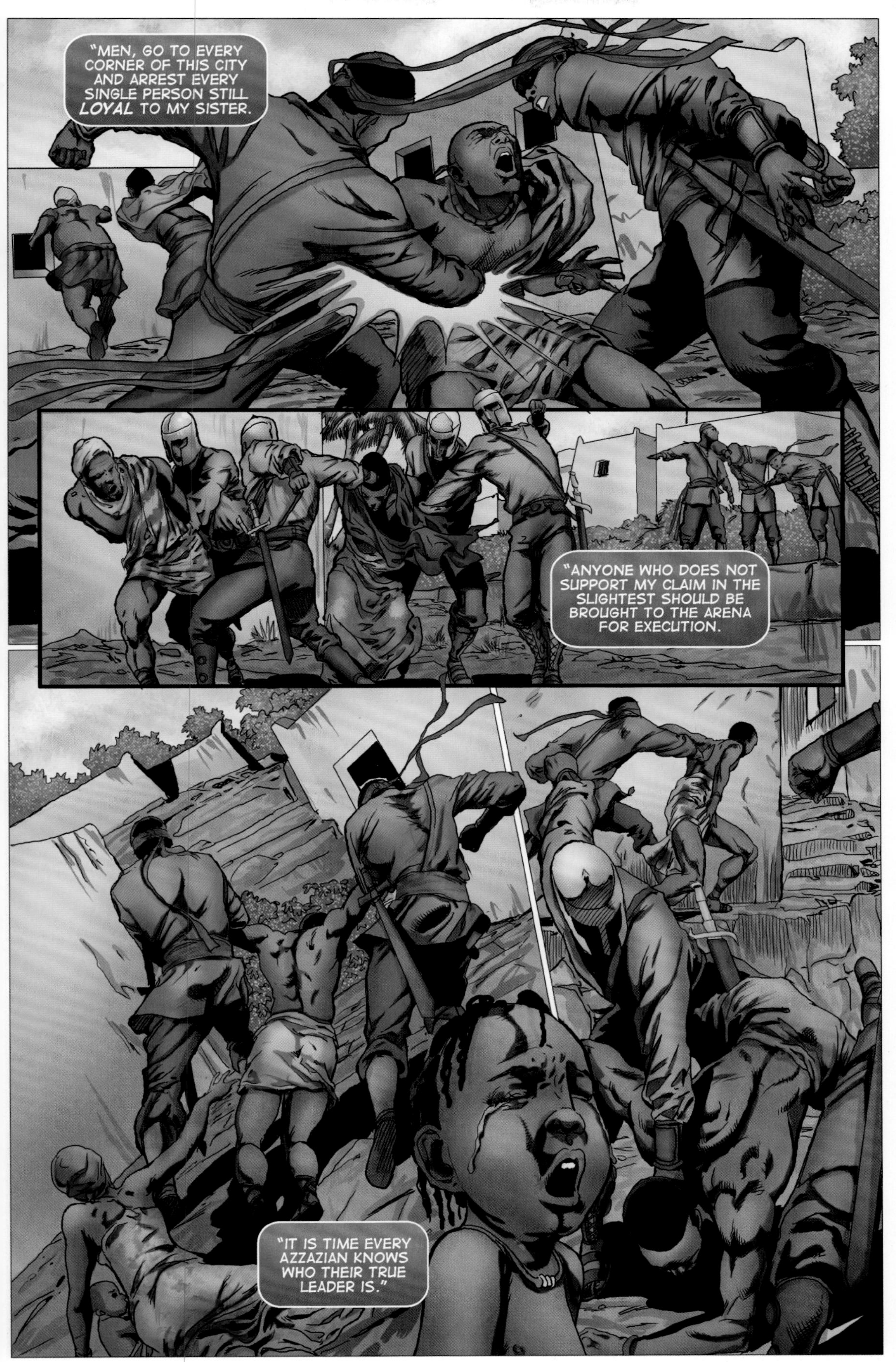
"MEN, GO TO EVERY CORNER OF THIS CITY AND ARREST EVERY SINGLE PERSON STILL *LOYAL* TO MY SISTER.
"ANYONE WHO DOES NOT SUPPORT MY CLAIM IN THE SLIGHTEST SHOULD BE BROUGHT TO THE ARENA FOR EXECUTION.
"IT IS TIME EVERY AZZAZIAN KNOWS WHO THEIR TRUE LEADER IS."

AGAIN.
MALIKA, I KNOW YOU ARE TRYING TO TEST YOUR *LIMITS* WITH THIS WEAPON. BUT YOU HAVE BEEN AT IT SINCE DAWN. PERHAPS--
I SAID AGAIN!

CLING
CLANG
CLING
CLINK

OMPFF!
URRGH!
RED KNIGHTS. THE ELITE OF THE RED RAVEN ARMY. YOU LOT CERTAINLY LIVE UP TO YOUR NAME. WELL...

SO
DO I!

ZZNNMMMMM
YOU MEN FOUGHT BRAVELY.
I THANK YOU FOR SPARRING WITH ME, BUT I THINK WE HAVE ALL HAD ENOUGH FOR NOW.
AMAZING STRENGTH. WITH MALIKA AT HER ***FULL POWER***, MAYBE ATTACKING HEAD ON IS NOT SUCH A CRAZY IDEA.
YOU MAY HAVE TRAINED HER FROM CHILDHOOD, ABDUL, BUT THIS IS DIFFERENT.
YOU SEE, WITH DRAGON'S DESTINY THE MORE DIRE THE SITUATION, THE MORE POWERFUL SHE BECOMES. MALIKA WAS HOLDING BACK.
SHE COULD HAVE WIPED US ALL OUT WITH THAT ATTACK.
THAT IS GOOD, IS IT NOT?
THIS NEW POWER IS THE SOLUTION.
NO.
IT IS A PROBLEM.

MALIKA...
MALIKA...
LISTEN TO MY VOICE.
THERE IS ANOTHER WAY.
MALIKA...
MALIKA.
MALIKA!
MALIKA!
MALIKA, IT IS I, BENGU.
MY APOLOGIES, BENGU. I WAS IN DEEP THOUGHT.

YOU SAW HIM IN YOUR SLEEP, DID YOU NOT? *ORIS*? YOU PASSED THE ***DRAGON TRIALS***.
THAT IS HOW YOU ARE ABLE TO WIELD DRAGON'S DESTINY.

HOW DID YOU KNOW?
I HAVE STUDIED ALL THE SACRED ATALIAN WRITINGS. WHAT MANY SAW AS MYTH, MY KING AND I KNEW TO BE TRUTH.
HE SPEAKS TO YOU, DOES HE NOT?

HIS WORDS ARE VAGUE AND INCOHERENT. BUT FROM WHAT I CAN UNDERSTAND, THEY CONFLICT WITH MY DESIRES.
HE WARNS ME TO SUBDUE MY RAGE AND TO FOCUS ON SAVING LIVES, INCLUDING THOSE OF MY ENEMIES, AS OPPOSED TO TAKING THEM.
MY PEOPLE CALL IT THE SPIRIT OF ORIS. OR MORE COMMONLY, THE ORIS SPIRIT.
OF WHAT USE IS ALL THIS POWER IF I CANNOT WIELD IT?

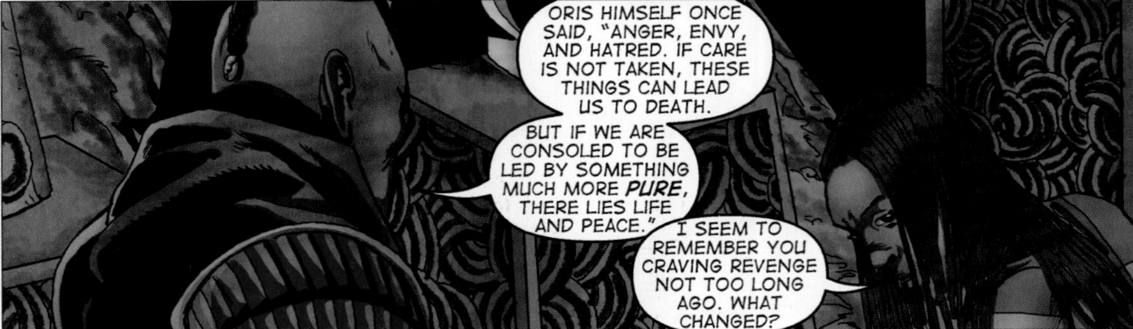
ORIS HIMSELF ONCE SAID, "ANGER, ENVY, AND HATRED. IF CARE IS NOT TAKEN, THESE THINGS CAN LEAD US TO DEATH.
BUT IF WE ARE CONSOLED TO BE LED BY SOMETHING MUCH MORE *PURE*, THERE LIES LIFE AND PEACE."
I SEEM TO REMEMBER YOU CRAVING REVENGE NOT TOO LONG AGO. WHAT CHANGED?

YOU ARE NOT THE ONLY ONE HE SPEAKS TO, MALIKA. AND I AM NOT ADVOCATING THAT WE SHOULD FORGO JUSTICE.
OUR KING DESERVES IT, AND YOUR PEOPLE NEED RESCUE. WHAT I SUGGEST IS WE CONSIDER OUR METHODS.
IF WE SIMPLY KILL EVERYONE IN OUR WAY, HOW WOULD THAT MAKE US ANY DIFFERENT FROM OUR ENEMIES?
WHAT WOULD YOU HAVE ME DO?
LISTEN. LET HIM GUIDE YOU.
IT IS WHAT BASS WOULD WANT.
YOUR TATTOO. WHAT DOES IT SYMBOLIZE?

A NOMAD VISITED ME SOME YEARS AGO. A VERY CURIOUS FELLOW HE WAS, BUT ALSO KNOWLEDGEABLE.
HIS WISDOM FASCINATED ME, SO WE QUICKLY BECAME FRIENDS.
ONE DAY AS WE DISCUSSED, I NOTICED THIS SYMBOL WAS ON ONE OF HIS ARTIFACTS, SO I ASKED HIM WHAT IT MEANT.
WHAT DID HE SAY IT MEANT?
IT MEANS--
MALIKA, FORGIVE ME FOR INTERRUPTING.
IT IS ALL RIGHT, ABDUL. YOUR INTERRUPTION IS ABOUT THE ONLY THING THAT FEELS NORMAL RIGHT NOW. WHAT TROUBLES YOU?
THE MEN ARE RESTLESS. ARE WE PROCEEDING AS PLANNED?
DO WE MARCH ON AZZAZ EVEN WITH OUR LIMITED NUMBERS?
YES. BUT WE MUST GO ABOUT THINGS A LITTLE DIFFERENTLY.

CHAPTER ELEVEN

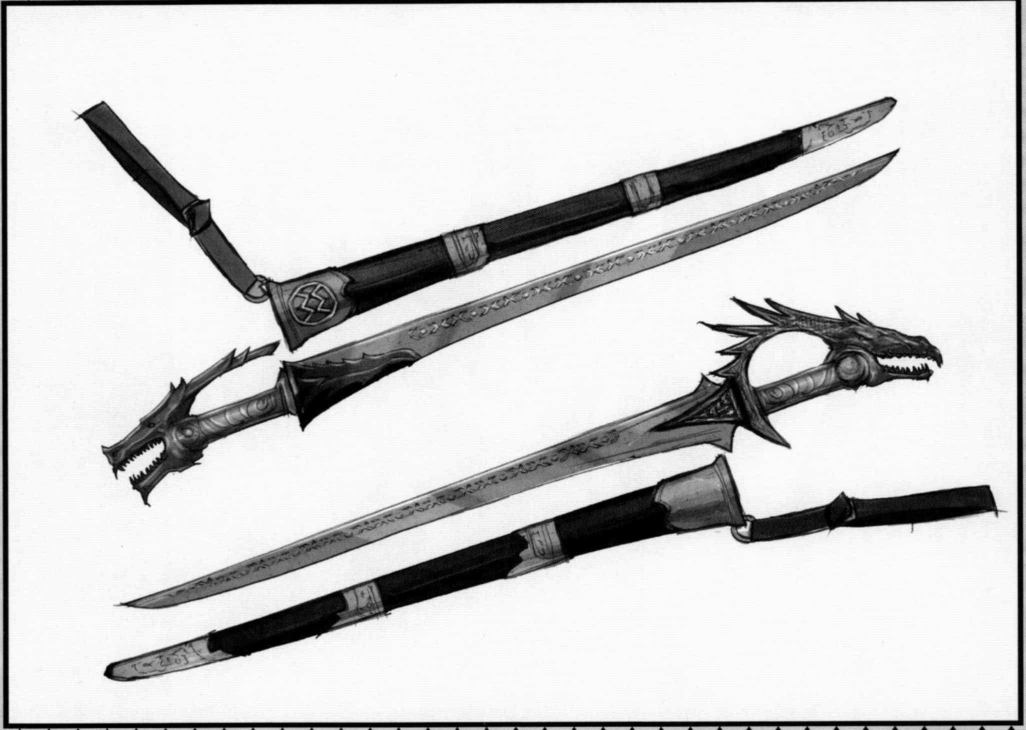

THE DRAGON SWORDS

"Dragon's Destiny and Dragon's Doom are two things that really start to push the *Malika* series into fantasy territory. The introduction of magical swords into the story was definitely exciting for me as a writer, but what was even more fun was the inspiration behind them: The Flyssa Sword, a Berber traditional blade that is specific to the Kablye people who reside in Algeria and Morocco. The blade of the Flyssa is usually decorated with symbolic glyphs and motifs, a concept you can see in the design of both Dragon's Destiny and Dragon's Doom."

—ROYE OKUPE

MY BROTHERS AND SISTERS, WELCOME TO A NEW AGE.
A NEW AZZAZ WHERE WEAKNESS HAS NO PLACE. WHERE WE TAKE WHAT WE WANT AND SUBDUE WHOMEVER WE WISH.
USING *FEAR*, WE WILL REIGN SUPREME ACROSS THE CONTINENT AND BRING PEACE TO A HOST OF SQUABBLING KINGDOMS.
BUT *REFORM* MUST START WITH US HERE AT HOME. FOR THE WEAK CANNOT RULE THE WEAK. WE WILL ROOT OUT DESPICABLE HABITS PASSED DOWN FROM A FAILED REGIME.
"SENTIMENT," "LOVE," "KINDNESS," SUCH THINGS HAVE NO PLACE IN AZZAZ.
WE RELY ON FORCE, STRENGTH, AND SHEER WILLPOWER. ANYTHING TO THE CONTRARY WILL BE ERADICATED.

NADIA! NADIA! NADIA!!
ALL HAIL QUEEN NADIA!
WHO WILL SAVE US NOW?
NO ONE. WE ARE DOOMED. FOR WE HAVE NO PLACE IN NADIA'S EMPIRE.
POOF

I HOPE THIS WORKS, MALIKA. WE GOT PAST THE CHECKPOINTS ONLY BECAUSE OF OUR SMALL NUMBERS. IF THIS FAILS, WE WILL BE SURROUNDED AND DESTROYED IN MINUTES.
THIS WILL WORK. NADIA IS TOO PROUD TO RESIST.
THE RAVENS?
THEY ARE IN POSITION. THERE ARE TUNNELS THAT EVEN NADIA IS NOT AWARE OF.
GENERAL ABDUL, QUEEN MALIKA!
KOBA! WE HEARD NOTHING FROM YOU AFTER YOU RODE TO SPY ON GENERAL CHENG. WE THOUGHT YOU WERE DEAD. HOW IS THIS POSSIBLE?
NOT YET, THANKFULLY. I RETURNED TO THE CATASTROPHE THAT IS NADIA. I SPENT DAYS SEARCHING FOR YOU, MY QUEEN, BUT IT WAS FUTILE.
I WAS JUST ABOUT TO SNEAK INTO THE CITY TO HELP THOSE STILL LOYAL TO YOU WHEN I SPOTTED YOU.
IT IS GOOD TO SEE YOU, KOBA.
MY QUEEN, MY DEEPEST APOLOGIES. I WAS NOT THERE TO PROTECT YOU. I SHOULD HA--
NONSENSE, KOBA. YOU ARE THE GREATEST SPY IN ALL OF AZZAZ. YOU WERE NEEDED ELSEWHERE.
DID YOU FIND OUT ANYTHING?

YES, GENERAL CHENG HAS FALLEN OUT WITH THE EMPEROR OF MING. HE HAS BEEN TOLD TO RETURN TO THE CAPITAL SEVERAL TIMES, BUT HE REFUSES.
EVEN WORSE IS THAT HIS MEN ARE TIRED AND HOMESICK.
MALIKA, WE CAN USE THIS.
WE WILL.
WE ARE ALMOST HOME, KEELA.
IMPOSSIBLE.
MALIKA! SHE IS HERE! SOUND THE ALARM! SECURE THE GATE!

POOM
POOM POOOOOMMMMMM
ARCHERS! PREPARE TO FIRE!!

VEEEM

KRA
KOOOOMMMM
RUN! EVACUATE THE TOWER!

BEGIN THE EXECU--
KRAKOOOMM

MY QUEEN, IT IS MALIKA. SHE IS HERE.

HOW?!

ALERT OUR MEN OUTSIDE THE CITY AT ONCE.

GO. NOW.

FEAR NOT, GENERAL. TODAY YOU WILL GET WHAT YOU WANT.

ABDUL! RAVENS!
NOW!
MALIKA! STICK TO THE PLAN. WE WILL HOLD THEM HERE!
VERY WELL! REMEMBER, LET US TRY NOT TO SPILL UNNECESSARY AZZAZIAN BLOOD TODAY!
TRY, I SHALL!
HAAA!
BOOM

SIR! A REPORT!
GO ON.
THERE HAS BEEN AN ATTACK ON THE CITY. IT IS MALIKA.
ALL UNITS WITHIN FIFTY KILOMETERS ARE TO REPORT BACK IMMEDIATELY.
YOU HEARD HIM. PREPARE TO MOVE OUT. WE RIDE FOR THE CITY IMMEDIATELY.
YOU WILL REMAIN LOYAL TO YOUR *TRUE* QUEEN. IF YOU BETRAY NADIA, I WILL KILL YOU MYSELF.

YOUR WORK HERE IS DONE, KEELA.

WARRIORS OF AZZAZ, I HAVE FOUGHT SIDE BY SIDE WITH MANY OF YOU. TOGETHER WE HAVE DEFENDED THIS EMPIRE.
I KNOW YOU FEEL LIKE YOU HAVE BETRAYED ME, BUT I ASSURE YOU, YOU HAVE NO REASON TO FEAR ME. FOR ALL THAT HAS HAPPENED WAS THROUGH NO FAULT OF YOURS.
I KNOW YOU ARE CONFUSED. BUT DEEP DOWN, I BELIEVE YOU KNOW WHO YOUR *TRUE* QUEEN IS.
LET ME RESTORE YOUR HOME BACK TO WHAT IT WAS BEFORE CHAOS REIGNED SUPREME.
FORGIVE US, MY QUEEN! WE THOUGHT YOU DEAD AND TRIED TO FORGE THE BEST WAY TO PEACE.
WE WERE COWARDS. WE SHOULD HAV--
NO, AMINA. YOU ARE HUMAN. YOU DID WHAT YOU FELT BEST. NOW I HAVE ONE MORE FAVOR TO ASK.
ANYTHING, MY QUEEN.
TAKE CARE OF KEELA FOR ME.
YES, MY QUEEN.

Art by Alitha E. Martinez

CHAPTER TWELVE

The Red Ravens

The Red Ravens, led by King Bass (AKA the WindMaker), are the protectors of Atala. As cool as their name is, there is more to it than meets the eye. And that "more" is a bird that's found only in Eastern and Southern Africa: the white-necked raven.

". . . As the Ravens fed upon the flesh of our elders' carcasses, the white patches on their necks became drenched in blood, turning it to red. To honor our fallen heroes, Bass named us, the group that fought back for freedom and justice, the Red Ravens. For these birds now carried the souls of our fallen leaders."

—From *The History of Atala*

DRAGON'S DESTINY? IMPOSSIBLE.
THE ANCIENT WRITINGS. THEY SAID IT WAS DESTROYED.
NADIA, I--
COUGH COUGH COUGH
...
YOU JUST REFUSE TO DIE.
I CAN SENSE THAT THE WEAPON IS ALL THAT IS KEEPING YOU UPRIGHT.

NADIA BAKWA! BY OUR LAWS, I CHALLENGE YOU TO SINGLE COMBAT FOR THE THRONE OF AZZAZ.
FOOL! YOU ARE ALREADY DOOMED.
WHY WOULD SHE--
I ACCEPT.
WHAT ARE YOU DOING? SHE IS SURROUNDED. WE CAN DESTROY HER AND BE DONE WITH IT. WE NEED TO SECURE THAT WEAPON.
STAY OUT OF THIS, CHENG. THIS IS AN AZZAZIAN MATTER NOW.
IMBECILE! YOU HAVE NO IDEA WHAT--
YOU OAF! IF YOU DO NOT THINK I CAN DEFEAT MY ALREADY DYING SISTER, THEN YOU CHOSE THE WRONG ALLY.
NOW RELAX IN THE COMFORT OF YOUR SAFETY AND DO WHAT YOU KNOW BEST. WATCH TRUE WARRIORS PROVIDE YOU WITH THE RESULTS YOU CRAVE.

CITIZENS OF AZZAZ, TONIGHT YOUR RULER WILL BE DECIDED. IN A BATTLE TO THE DEATH!
THIS IS BETWEEN YOU AND ME NOW, NADIA. LEAVE EVERYONE ELSE OUT OF IT.
DO IT.
MPOOM

DESTROY THEM!
POOOOMM
POOM
POOOOOM-M
HALT!
MALIKA... OUR QUEEN FIGHTS FOR US.

IS THIS NOT FITTING?
WHAT?
ABDUL MAY HAVE TRAINED YOU IN THE WAYS OF BATTLE STRATEGY, POLITICS, AND RULE...
...BUT IN THIS VERY ARENA, I TAUGHT YOU ALL YOU KNOW ABOUT HAND-TO-HAND COMBAT.
YOUR POINT?
THE CRUCIBLE THAT SHAPED US INTO WARRIORS WILL NOW BECOME YOUR TOMB.
DO YOU EVEN KNOW WHAT THAT WEAPON IS?
TRUE POWER.

TWOOOM
DIE!!!
THWAKOOOOM

CLANK
CLANK
WAM

KRAK
KOOOOM

WHAT IS SO FUNNY?
YOU ARE SO PETTY. ALLOWING CHENG TO MANIPULATE YOU WITH THAT WEAPON.
AND YET YOU HAVE THE GALL TO SPEAK OF WEAKNESS.
I MOURNED YOU, WEPT FOR YOU. AND FOR WHAT? FOR YOU TO COME BACK AND BETRAY YOUR OWN *BLOOD?!*

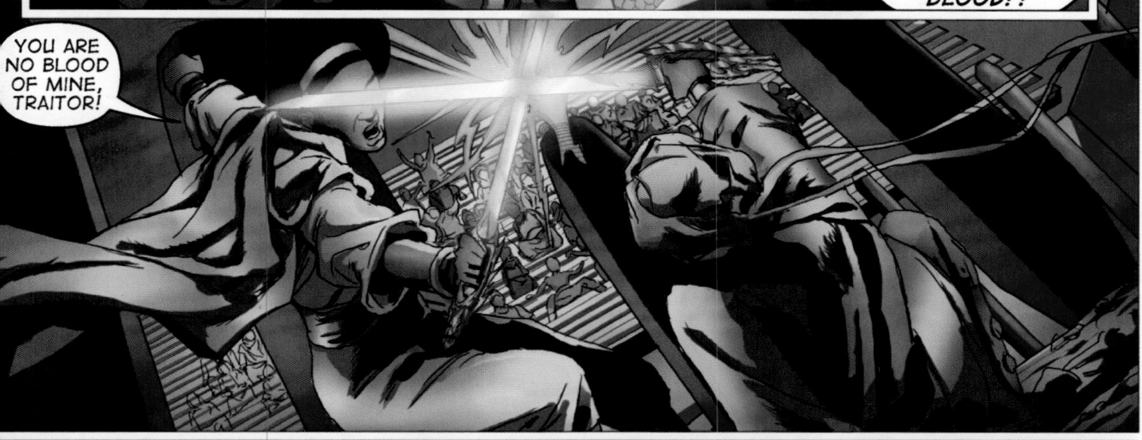
YOU ARE NO BLOOD OF MINE, TRAITOR!

OOMPPF!

SWOOOP
WAKOOM
TWOK
ARGH!

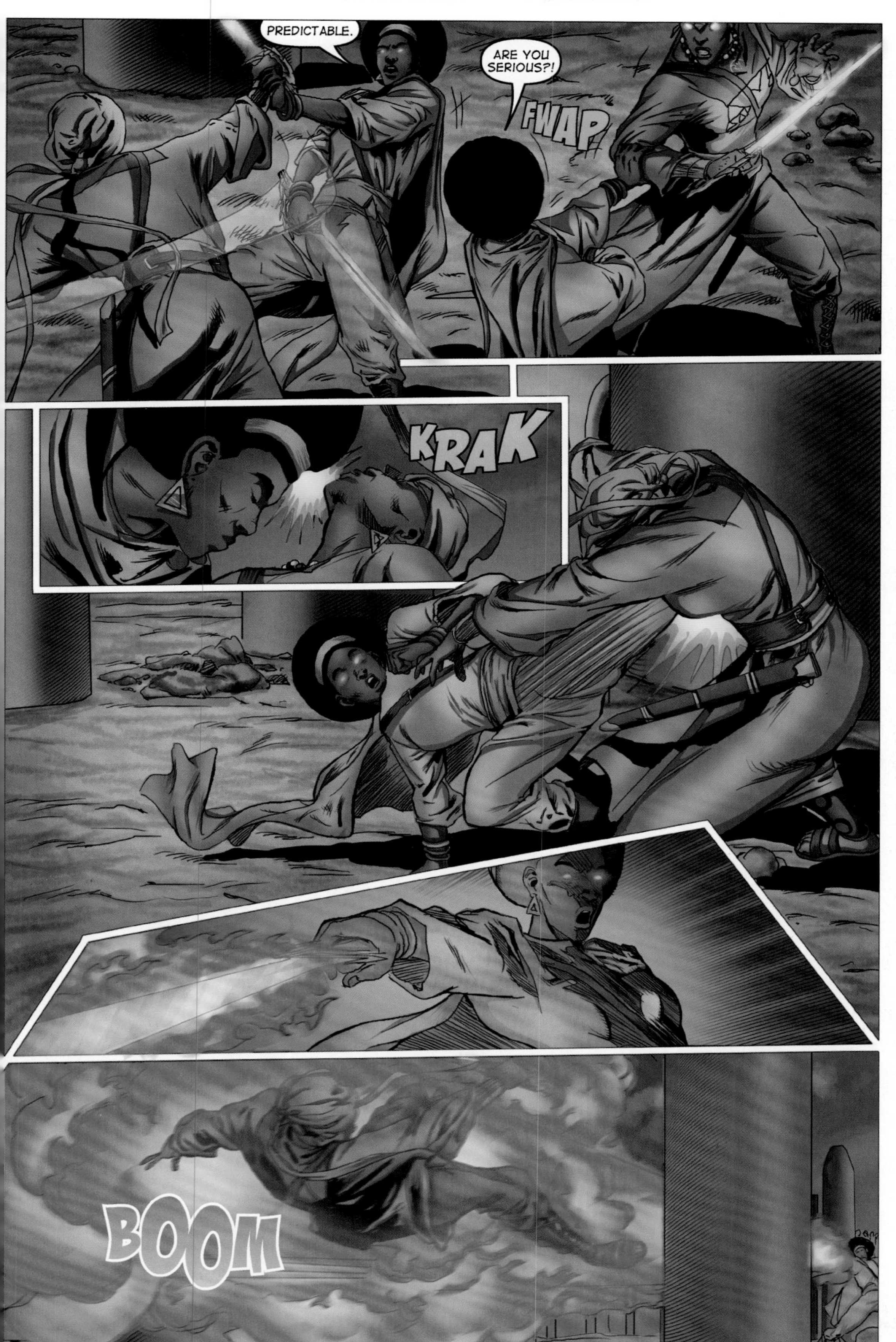
PREDICTABLE.
ARE YOU SERIOUS?!
FWAP
KRAK
BOOM

WE BELIEVE IN YOU, QUEEN MALIKA!
YOU WILL ALWAYS BE OUR QUEEN!
MALIKA!
MALIKA!
MALIKA!
KROOM
IS THAT SO?!
NO!!!
RGGHHAAAAAA!!
RGGHHHH...

AARRGH!!
TWOOOOOOM
MALIKA, RISE.
WHY SHOULD I? YOU ABANDONED ME.
MALIKA, MY FATHER AND I WERE SENT AS GUARDIANS TO EARTH BY THE ONE WHO HAS NO RIVAL NOR EQUAL. THE ONE WHO REIGNS FOREVER.
I COULD NOT ABANDON YOU EVEN IF I DESIRED TO.
THEN TELL ME, ORIS, WHY HAS IT BEEN SO DIFFICULT TO HEAR YOU?
BECAUSE YOU FOCUS ONLY ON WHAT YOU WANT ME TO SAY. NOT WHAT YOU NEED TO HEAR.
YOU KNOW WHAT YOU NEED TO DO.

I DO NOT KNOW IF I CAN.
FOR THE SAKE OF YOUR SISTER, YOUR PEOPLE, AND YOUR WORLD. YOU MUST.

I HOPE YOU ARE NOT DEAD. I AM BEGINNING TO ENJOY THIS.

NADIA, PLEASE. STOP THIS! YOU ARE NOT IN CONTROL!
YOU THINK I AM BEING *MANIPULATED?* THIS WEAPON FEEDS ON MY RAGE. I HAVE NEVER FELT MORE ALIVE.
WE LOVED EACH OTHER DEARLY! DOES THAT MEAN NOTHING TO YOU?! I REFUSE TO BELIEVE THAT THIS IS WHAT YOU HAVE BECOME!

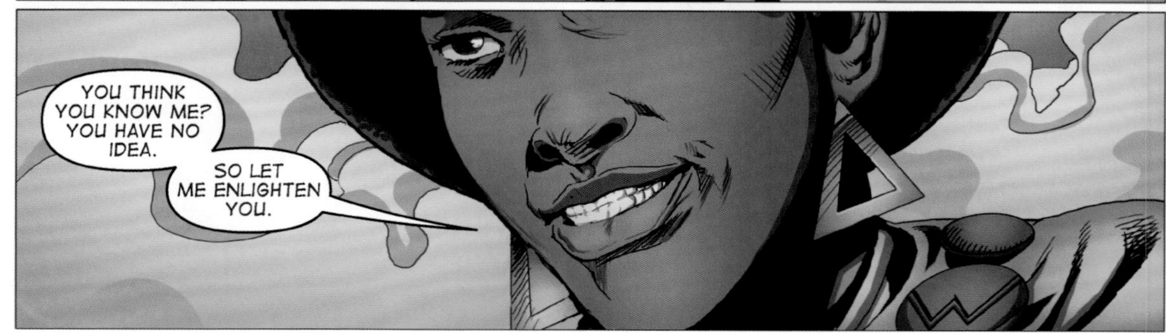
YOU THINK YOU KNOW ME? YOU HAVE NO IDEA.
SO LET ME ENLIGHTEN YOU.

"AFTER YOU AND YOUR MOTHER LEFT ME FOR DEAD, ALL I COULD THINK ABOUT WAS HOW MUCH I WANTED YOU BOTH TO SUFFER.
"AND AS FATE WOULD HAVE IT, I WOULD GET MY CHANCE...
"THE OLON JIN.
"THEY OFFERED TO USE *DARK MAGIC* TO MAKE ME *WHOLE*...
"AT FIRST I REFUSED FERVENTLY. I REMEMBERED THE FRIGHTENING STORIES WE WERE TOLD AS CHILDREN ABOUT THE OLON JIN.
"SO THEY OFFERED ME A LITTLE *TASTE* OF THEIR POWER.
"A CHANCE TO TRY OUT MY RESTORED BODY AND DO AS I PLEASED WITH IT.
"I KNEW EXACTLY WHAT I WANTED TO DO NEXT."

NADIA, THAT POWER COMES AT A COST! HOW COULD YOU SELL YOUR SOUL TO THE OLON JIN?
MY SOUL? NO. MY CONSCIENCE? YES.
I WAS TIRED OF IT ALL. TIRED OF SENTIMENT, LOVE, KINDNESS. ALL THE EMOTIONS THAT WEIGH US DOWN AS HUMANS.
WE WERE ALWAYS TOLD BY FATHER THAT WE AZZAZIANS WERE BORN TO BE THE APEX OF ALL WARRIORS.
BUT TO BECOME THE ULTIMATE WARRIOR, ONE MUST UNTETHER THEMSELVES ENTIRELY FROM USELESS EMOTIONS.
RAGE, FURY, WRATH. ONLY WHEN YOU MASTER THESE CAN YOU EMBRACE TRUE POWER.
ALL THIS... FOR THE THRONE?
ALL THIS FOR MY BIRTHRIGHT!
YOU TOOK EVERYTHING AWAY FROM ME, SO I TOOK EVERYTHING AWAY FROM YOU. OR AT LEAST I TRIED.
YOU DID WHAT?

"SURPRISINGLY, I DID NOT EVEN HESITATE...
"I DID IT. I KILLED OUR MOTHER.
"YES, MALIKA.
"IT WAS I, DISGUISED AS THE 'SONGHAI ASSASSIN' THAT HELPED TRIGGER THE SECOND SONGHAI WAR.
"A WAR THAT WOULD CRUSH THE KINGDOM YOU INHERITED. OR SO I THOUGHT.
"UNTIL YOU EXCEEDED EXPECTATIONS YET AGAIN.
"NOT ONLY DID YOU DEFEAT THE SONGHAI COWARDS, YOU ALSO UNIFIED AZZAZ AND THE NEIGHBORING KINGDOMS, TURNING IT INTO THE EMPIRE IT IS TODAY!
"KILLING JOHARA BROUGHT ME FREEDOM, SO I GLADLY ACCEPTED THE OFFER FROM THE OLON JIN.
"FATALLY WOUNDED, I HAD TO BE SUSPENDED IN DEEP SLEEP FOR YEARS WHILE THE DARK MAGIC HEALED ME.
"ONCE I AWOKE, I SLOWLY BEGAN TO INCITE AND TRAIN THE REBELS, AWAITING MY MOMENT.
"WHEN YOU DECLARED WAR ON MING AND THE FIVE LOST FAITH IN YOU, I KNEW IT WAS TIME."

TIME TO EMBRACE TRUE POWER.
YOU STILL THINK YOU KNOW ME, SISTER? OR DO YOU NOW KNOW I WILL DO WHATEVER IT TAKES TO RECLAIM WHAT IS RIGHTFULLY MINE?
HOW... HOW COULD YOU?
ENOUGH BANTER.
NOW, HOW ABOUT YOU ATTACK ME WITH SOME MORE OF THOSE PREDICTABLE TECHNIQUES I TAUGHT YOU.
I PROMISE TO PUT YOU OUT OF YOUR MISERY. QUICKLY.
MALIKA, SHE IS LOST TO USEH. HE MUST BE STOPPED.
NOW IS THE TIME.
KUNG FU?
INTERESTING, I SEE YOUR HUSBAND TAUGHT YOU THE WAYS OF HIS MONK INSTRUCTORS.

LET US SEE IF HE WAS A BETTER TEACHER THAN ME!
HAAA!
SKLINGG
STAY STILL!
TRY TO KEEP UP, SISTER.

HOW LONG DO YOU THINK YOU CAN KEEP THIS UP BEFORE THE POISON MAKES YOUR HEART GIVE OUT?!

WAKOOOM

LONG ENOUGH TO PUT YOU IN YOUR PLACE.

YOU WERE NEVER DESTINED TO RULE...
I SAID QUIET!
WHOOOOM
NEVER FIT FOR THE THRONE...
OMMPPFFF!
YOU WERE TOO WEAK. ALWAYS ANGRY. YOU NEVER THOUGHT THINGS THROUGH.

ARGGHHH!!!!
I HATE YOU!!!
USEH, I WILL NOT LET YOU DESTROY THIS WORLD AGAIN.
YOUR RAGE IS ALREADY DESTROYING HER BODY.
ONCE IT HAS CONSUMED HER, YOU WILL BE FORCED TO FREE HER SOUL.
YOU CANNOT STOP ME, BROTHER!
SO IT MAY BE. BUT THIS WORLD IS FILLED WITH ANGER, RAGE, GREED, AND JEALOUSY.
I WILL FIND ANOTHER, AND THEN ANOTHER. AND ONCE THIS WORLD IS FILLED WITH ENOUGH RAGE AND CHAOS, I WILL BE FREE TO RETURN!
DARKNESS WILL FILL THE EARTH AGAIN.
MARK MY WORDS, I WILL NEVER ALLOW IT. EVEN IF I HAVE TO PRESERVE MY CURRENT VESSEL FOR CENTURIES, I WILL ALWAYS BE HERE TO STOP YOU.
OOOMMMM

WAAM
AND MOST OF ALL...
YOU WILL NEVER BE AS GOOD AS I AM.
HOW DARE YOU!!!

ARGGHH--
RGGGGHHHH!!
MALIKA...
I...
TH--

SWINNNNZZZ
NADIA...
NO...
NOOOOOO!!!!!
RAVENS! SECURE DRAGON'S DOOM. AZZAZIANS! WITH ME!
NADIA HAS FAILED US. OUR LORD WILL NOT BE PLEASED.
THIS JUST *DELAYS* THE INEVITABLE. WE WILL FIND ANOTHER.
I AM SO SORRY, MY DEAR SISTER.

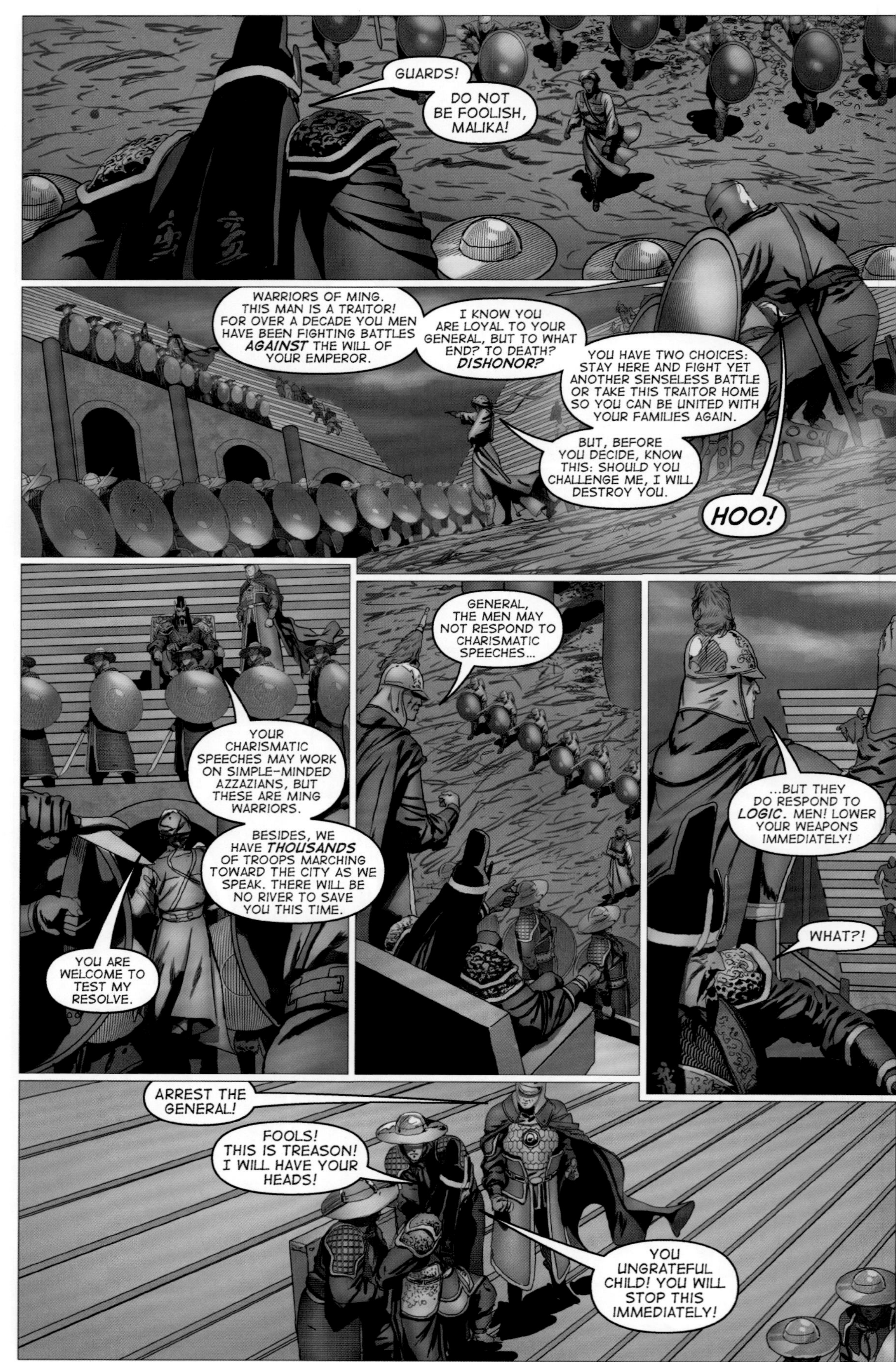
GUARDS!
DO NOT BE FOOLISH, MALIKA!
WARRIORS OF MING. THIS MAN IS A TRAITOR! FOR OVER A DECADE YOU MEN HAVE BEEN FIGHTING BATTLES *AGAINST* THE WILL OF YOUR EMPEROR.
I KNOW YOU ARE LOYAL TO YOUR GENERAL, BUT TO WHAT END? TO DEATH? *DISHONOR?*
YOU HAVE TWO CHOICES: STAY HERE AND FIGHT YET ANOTHER SENSELESS BATTLE OR TAKE THIS TRAITOR HOME SO YOU CAN BE UNITED WITH YOUR FAMILIES AGAIN.
BUT, BEFORE YOU DECIDE, KNOW THIS: SHOULD YOU CHALLENGE ME, I WILL DESTROY YOU.
HOO!
YOUR CHARISMATIC SPEECHES MAY WORK ON SIMPLE-MINDED AZZAZIANS, BUT THESE ARE MING WARRIORS.
BESIDES, WE HAVE *THOUSANDS* OF TROOPS MARCHING TOWARD THE CITY AS WE SPEAK. THERE WILL BE NO RIVER TO SAVE YOU THIS TIME.
YOU ARE WELCOME TO TEST MY RESOLVE.
GENERAL, THE MEN MAY NOT RESPOND TO CHARISMATIC SPEECHES...
...BUT THEY DO RESPOND TO *LOGIC*. MEN! LOWER YOUR WEAPONS IMMEDIATELY!
WHAT?!
ARREST THE GENERAL!
FOOLS! THIS IS TREASON! I WILL HAVE YOUR HEADS!
YOU UNGRATEFUL CHILD! YOU WILL STOP THIS IMMEDIATELY!

ON BEHALF OF THE MING DYNASTY, ALLOW ME TO OFFER OUR DEEPEST APOLOGIES FOR THE HORRORS THE GENERAL HAS CAUSED.
JUST GET HIM OUT OF MY SIGHT BEFORE I KILL HIM.
MALIKA!
ABDUL I--
MALIKA!
I HAVE YOU.
TAKE ME TO THEM.
MALIKA! MY QUEEN. PLEASE, HAVE MERCY. WE WERE FOOLED. I BEG OF YOU. PLEASE SHOW US MERCY.
PLEASE, MALIKA! HAVE MERCY!

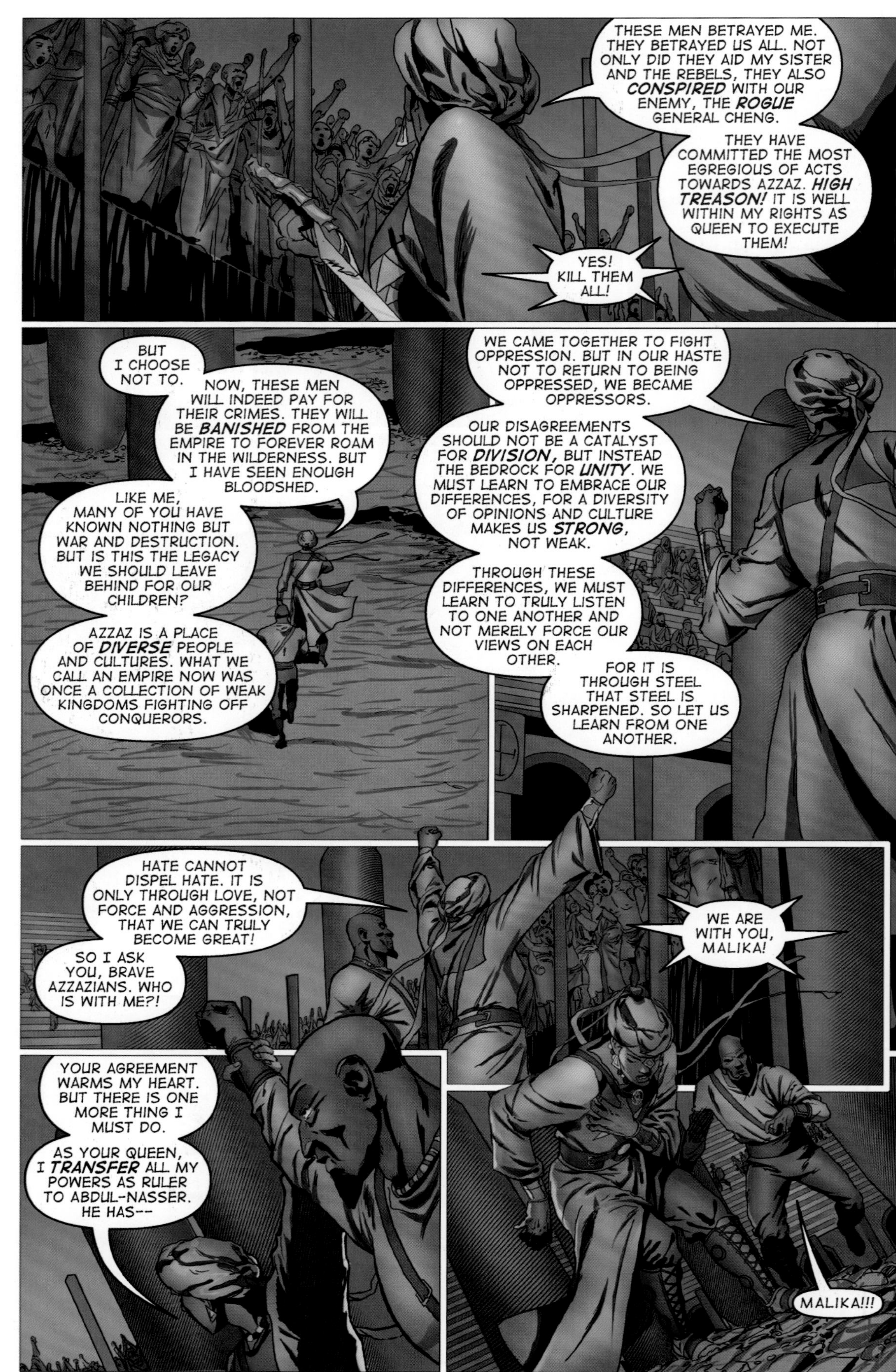

THESE MEN BETRAYED ME. THEY BETRAYED US ALL. NOT ONLY DID THEY AID MY SISTER AND THE REBELS, THEY ALSO CONSPIRED WITH OUR ENEMY, THE ROGUE GENERAL CHENG.
THEY HAVE COMMITTED THE MOST EGREGIOUS OF ACTS TOWARDS AZZAZ. HIGH TREASON! IT IS WELL WITHIN MY RIGHTS AS QUEEN TO EXECUTE THEM!
YES! KILL THEM ALL!
BUT I CHOOSE NOT TO.
NOW, THESE MEN WILL INDEED PAY FOR THEIR CRIMES. THEY WILL BE BANISHED FROM THE EMPIRE TO FOREVER ROAM IN THE WILDERNESS. BUT I HAVE SEEN ENOUGH BLOODSHED.
LIKE ME, MANY OF YOU HAVE KNOWN NOTHING BUT WAR AND DESTRUCTION. BUT IS THIS THE LEGACY WE SHOULD LEAVE BEHIND FOR OUR CHILDREN?
AZZAZ IS A PLACE OF DIVERSE PEOPLE AND CULTURES. WHAT WE CALL AN EMPIRE NOW WAS ONCE A COLLECTION OF WEAK KINGDOMS FIGHTING OFF CONQUERORS.
WE CAME TOGETHER TO FIGHT OPPRESSION. BUT IN OUR HASTE NOT TO RETURN TO BEING OPPRESSED, WE BECAME OPPRESSORS.
OUR DISAGREEMENTS SHOULD NOT BE A CATALYST FOR DIVISION, BUT INSTEAD THE BEDROCK FOR UNITY. WE MUST LEARN TO EMBRACE OUR DIFFERENCES, FOR A DIVERSITY OF OPINIONS AND CULTURE MAKES US STRONG, NOT WEAK.
THROUGH THESE DIFFERENCES, WE MUST LEARN TO TRULY LISTEN TO ONE ANOTHER AND NOT MERELY FORCE OUR VIEWS ON EACH OTHER.
FOR IT IS THROUGH STEEL THAT STEEL IS SHARPENED. SO LET US LEARN FROM ONE ANOTHER.
HATE CANNOT DISPEL HATE. IT IS ONLY THROUGH LOVE, NOT FORCE AND AGGRESSION, THAT WE CAN TRULY BECOME GREAT!
SO I ASK YOU, BRAVE AZZAZIANS. WHO IS WITH ME?!
WE ARE WITH YOU, MALIKA!
YOUR AGREEMENT WARMS MY HEART. BUT THERE IS ONE MORE THING I MUST DO.
AS YOUR QUEEN, I TRANSFER ALL MY POWERS AS RULER TO ABDUL-NASSER. HE HAS--
MALIKA!!!

MALIKA!
MALIKA, PLEASE HOLD ON. TELL ME WHA--
IT IS ALL RIGHT, ABDUL. IT IS TIME.
LISTEN TO ME CAREFULLY. YOU MUST BURY ME WITH DRAGON'S DESTINY. IN A PLACE NO ONE CAN FIND.
BUT WHERE?
WHERE BASS AND I FIRST MET. YOU MUST DO IT ALONE.
I UNDERSTAND. I WILL, I PROMISE.
DRAGON'S DOOM...TELL THE RAVENS...THEY MUST...
MALIKA...MALIKA... MALIKA!

CHAPTER THIRTEEN (EPILOGUE)

The YouNeek YouNiverse

"What we are trying to do over the next few years is create a compelling and immersive universe with our own twist. How? Well, the YouNeek YouNiverse is a massive, interconnected universe of sci-fi, fantasy, and superhero content spread across multiple timelines with stories told from an African perspective. Is this ambitious? Yes. Is it impossible? Not at all. With this monumental partnership with Dark Horse and the impeccable history, support, and infrastructure they bring to the table, we will finally be able to achieve our ultimate goal: create, for a global audience, content that empowers African creatives and storytelling."

—Roye Okupe

BEIJING.
MING DYNASTY.
GENERAL CHENG, YOUR ACTIONS OVER THE LAST SEVERAL YEARS HAVE BEEN A COMPLETE DISGRACE TO THE MING DYNASTY.
WORSE, YOU REFUSED TO HEED THE INSTRUCTIONS OF YOUR EMPEROR. WHAT DO YOU HAVE TO SAY FOR YOURSELF?
MY LOYALTY IS TO MING. I REGRET NOTHING.
YOUR LOYALTY IS TO YOURSELF, AND YOU HAVE ACCOMPLISHED NOTHING. YOU WERE TO WORK WITH AND LEARN FROM THE ATALIANS, BUT YOU CHOSE SUBJUGATION INSTEAD OF COHABITATION.
AND INSTEAD OF RETURNING HOME AFTER YOUR FAILURE, YOU DECIDED TO DECLARE WAR ON AZZAZ IN MY NAME, EVEN THOUGH I GAVE NO SUCH ORDER.
民事維難
YOU ARE CORRECT. I AM LOYAL TO MYSELF. BUT IT IS ONLY BECAUSE YOU ARE A WEAK COWARD WHO LACKS AMBITION.

GO AHEAD! KILL ME! I WILL TAKE SOLACE IN DESTROYING MALIKA AND HER SPINELESS LOVER!
I SHOULD EXECUTE YOU. BUT I WON'T.
IS THIS ANOTHER ONE OF YOUR DECISIONS THAT REQUIRES SENSELESS PONDERING? OR ARE YOU SIMPLY TOO WEAK TO SULLY YOUR HANDS?
NOT QUITE. I HAVE SOMETHING BETTER IN MIND. MY FATHER WAS AGAINST THIS, BUT IT'S TIME YOU LEARNED THE TRUTH.
WHAT TRUTH?

WE ARE BROTHERS, CHENG.
WELL, HALF-BROTHERS. SEEING AS YOU WERE BORN OUT OF WEDLOCK. TO AVOID EMBARRASSMENT, YOU WERE CAST OUT. ABANDONED.
IMPOSSIBLE! LIAR!

IT'S THE TRUTH, AND YOU KNOW IT. BECAUSE RIGHT NOW YOU ARE WONDERING IF MY FATHER RESCUED YOU FROM THE SLUMS OUT OF GUILT.
HE DID. AND TO AVOID A DISPUTE OVER THE THRONE, HE LIED TO YOU. IF ONLY HE COULD SEE THE IRONY NOW.

PONDER THAT WHILE YOU SPEND THE REST OF YOUR LIFE IN A DARK HOLE.
TAKE HIM AWAY.

REST WELL, MY QUEEN.

KOOOOOMMMMMMMMMM
WHERE... WHERE AM I?
LAGOON CITY, LAGOS, NIGERIA. 2003.
SIR, I FOUND SOMEONE!
WHO ARE YOU? AND WHERE AM I?
I AM DR. WILLIAMS AND I PROMISE, WE MEAN YOU NO HARM.
I...
MEN, HELP ME. SHE NEEDS MEDICAL ATTENTION IMMEDIATELY.

THE NEXT DAY.
HMMPPFFF!
IT'S OKAY, MALIKA. YOU'RE SAFE.
YOU AGAIN? WHERE AM I? AND HOW DO YOU KNOW MY NAME?
THAT SYMBOL. IT'S UNMISTAKABLE. AND YOU'RE SAFE. THIS IS MY LAB. I BROUGHT YOU HERE AFTER YOU PASSED OUT LAST NIGHT.
"LAB"?
IT MAKES SENSE THAT YOU WOULDN'T UNDERSTAND WHAT THAT MEANS. CARBON DATING DETERMINED THAT THE CRYPT YOU EMERGED FROM WAS BUILT SOMETIME DURING THE FIFTEENTH CENTURY.
I STILL DO NOT UNDERSTAND.
YOU HAVE BEEN BURIED FOR ABOUT FIVE HUNDRED YEARS, MALIKA.

ORIS, HE MUST HAVE PUT ME TO SLEEP ALL THESE YEARS. BUT WHY?
SLEEP? DO YOU MEAN SOME SORT OF *SUSPENDED ANIMATION?* MAGNIFICENT!
EXCEPT... DRAGON'S DOOM. OH, NO.
I MUST GO. HOW DO I GET OUT OF HERE?
MALIKA, PLEASE. YOU HAVE TO REST.
IF WHAT YOU ARE TELLING ME IS TRUE, THEN WE HAVE NO IDEA WHAT WE ARE DEALING WITH.
AND THAT'S NOT EVEN MY MAIN CONCERN.
MALIKA, YOU'RE *PREGNANT*.
WHAT? MY CHILD...
IT SURVIVED?
I...I JUST ASSUMED...
ALIVE AND WELL. I'M NOT SURE HOW THAT'S POSSIBLE EITHER, BUT IT'S TRUE. I ALSO NEED TO RUN SOME TESTS TO MAKE SURE EVERYTHING ELSE IS ALL RIGHT WITH YOU.
VERY WELL.
BASS...
THAT NECKLACE. WHERE DID YOU GET IT?

IT WAS A GIFT. WHY?
IT'S HOW WE FOUND YOU. IT SHARES THE EXACT SAME PROPERTIES AS A RARE ORE I'VE BEEN SEARCHING FOR.
I BELIEVE IT CAN SAVE A LOT OF LIVES. BUT WE CAN DISCUSS THAT LATER.
OH, AND ONE MORE THING.
YES?
MY SON *WALE* SNUCK IN HERE LAST NIGHT. HE DREW THIS WHILE YOU WERE ASLEEP.
I'M NOT SURE WHERE HE SAW THIS.
IT IS A TATTOO.
BEAUTIFUL! WHAT DOES IT MEAN? IT LOOKS LIKE A COMBINATION OF THE LETTERS "E", "X", AND MAYBE AN--
IT MEANS *FAITH*.
CONTINUES IN VOLUME 2!

This page and facing page: Art by Chima Kalu, with colors by Raphael Kazeem

This piece is called "Malika Through the Years," as we can see images of her as a mature queen (left), young princess (center), and teenage princess (right).

MALIKA
Warrior Queen

"DRAGON TRIALS"

CREATOR AND WRITER
ROYE OKUPE

ART
CHIMA KALU

COLORS
OSAS ASEMOTA

LETTERS
SPOOF ANIMATION

COVER ART (PREVIOUS PAGE) AND CONCEPT ART
GODWIN AKPAN

BONUS STORY UNIQUE TO THIS EDITION!

THE DIVINE ONES

"The all-powerful Divine Ones. Our dieties. Said to have migrated from what is now the Oyo Kingdom, the Divine Ones comprise Atala, along with his two sons Oris and Useh. A family of dragon riders, as they were called back then, the Divine Ones were the most powerful beings of their era. But like most all-powerful families of gods, this power would cause dissent amongst their ranks. And this dissent came in form of what we Atalians call: the "rage of Useh."

You see, back then as it is now, it was very common for offspring to worship their fathers, seeking attention and acceptance. Year after year, both Oris and Useh made sacrifices to please their father, Atala. However, Useh, ever the eager one, took many shortcuts in his ways. This displeased Atala, who began to favor the more forebearing and wise Oris. Years passed and Oris became the clear favorite of the two, further driving Useh toward rage, jealousy, and bitterness. And then came the tipping point. For his continued excellence, Oris was granted Dragon's Destiny, Atala's most prized possession and perhaps the most powerful weapon ever created.

Following this event, Useh went mad with rage. So much so that he manifested it as raw energy with the help of dark magic. Next, Useh used this new power to craft his own blade—a blade he called Dragon's Doom. Its power rivaled that of Dragon's Destiny. But Useh did not stop there. With Dragon's Doom, he set his sights on his own father. Atala was so weakened in his heart by his son's betrayal, that he refused to fight him when confronted. Useh killed Atala without hesitation. Without a shadow of doubt, I believe Atala allowed this to happen. I can only hope that one day we will know why."

—FROM *THE HISTORY OF ATALA*

WHAT... WHAT IS THIS...
WHERE AM I?
CALM YOUR MIND, MALIKA. YOU ARE SAFE. JUST--
WHO ARE YOU? AND WHY DO I FEEL...
MY MIND... IT FEELS...
ALL WILL BE EXPLAINED.
FOR NOW YOU MUST CALM YOUR MIND OTHERWISE THIS PLACE WILL *CRUMBLE.*
AZZAZ... MY HOME, MY PEOPLE... THEY ARE IN DANGER. I MUST...
ARGH!!!
GRRGRGRG
GRGRGRRR
MALIKA, YOU HAVE EXPERIENCED A VERY TRAUMATIC EVENT.
IF YOU CANNOT FIND TRANQUILITY IN THIS PLACE, ALL WILL BE LOST.
...
YES. JUST LIKE THAT. FIND YOUR CENTER. FIND YOUR PEACE.

WHAT IS THIS PLACE?
THE KINGDOM OF ATALA? HOW DID WE GET SO FAR AWAY FROM AZZAZ?
WE ARE NOT IN ATALA. OR EVEN ANYWHERE CLOSE TO YOUR EMPIRE.
WE ARE IN YOUR MIND, MALIKA.
WHAT?! HOW IS THAT EVEN POSSI--
ZING
ARGH!!!
YOUR MIND IS STILL TRYING TO COME TO TERMS WITH THE TRAUMA YOU EXPERIENCED IN THE PHYSICAL WORLD.
FOR THE SAKE OF WHAT IS TO COME, I HAD TO FRAGMENT YOUR THOUGHTS.
THAT IS WHY YOU ARE CURRENTLY EXPERIENCING GAPS IN YOUR MEMORIES.
END THIS! I WANT NO PART OF THIS MINDLESS GAME. MY PEOPLE NEED ME.
I WILL NOT FORCE MY WILL UPON YOU. THOUGH I COULD. BUT I URGE YOU TO LISTEN TO WHAT I HAVE TO SAY BEFORE YOU DECIDE.

YOU KNOW EXACTLY WHO I AM.
I STILL DO NOT KNOW WHO YOU ARE.
ORIS? WHAT IS AN ATALIAN DEITY DOING IN MY MIND?
THE KING OF YOUR ATALIAN ALLIES TO THE SOUTH, THE ONE THEY CALL THE *WINDMAKER*, BROUGHT MY SWORD TO YOU.
DRAGON'S DESTINY.
WHAT YOU THOUGHT WAS MYTH HAS BECOME YOUR REALITY. THE SWORD CARRIES MY SPIRIT.
THE MOMENT YOU WIELDED IT IN YOUR WORLD, IT CHOSE YOU.
I DO NOT REMEMBER ANYTHING CHANGING THEN.
TRUE CHANGE DOES NOT REQUIRE THEATRICALITY TO PROVE ITS MERITS.
HMPF CRYPTIC PROVERBS. NOW I TRULY BELIEVE YOU INDEED ARE A DEITY.
IT IS GOOD TO SEE YOU ARE FINALLY FINDING YOURSELF IN THIS PLACE. YOU WILL NEED YOUR WIT IF YOU ARE TO FACE WHAT IS COMING.
YOU HAVE MY ATTENTION.

EVIL HAS RETURNED TO YOUR WORLD.
IF LEFT UNCHECKED, ITS RAGE WILL CONSUME THE ENTIRE PLANET.
JUST LIKE IT DID IN MY TIME ON EARTH.
USEH...
THE WINDMAKER TOLD YOU BUT A FRACTION OF THE EVIL MY BROTHER BROUGHT TO YOUR WORLD.
HIS KNOWLEDGE WAS LIMITED BY WHAT WAS PASSED DOWN THROUGH ATALIAN HISTORIANS.
BUT I ASSURE YOU, USEH IS FAR WORSE THAN YOU CAN EVER IMAGINE.
HOW HAS HE RETURNED? YOU DEFEATED HIM.
LIKE ME, USEH'S SPIRIT DWELLS IN HIS SWORD, DRAGON'S DOOM. SOMEONE IN YOUR WORLD HAS ACCESSED ITS POWERS, ALLOWING THEMSELVES TO BE CONSUMED BY USEH'S SPIRIT. THE ENTIRE WORLD IS IN DANGER.
MY FIRST RESPONSIBILITY IS TO AZZAZ. I AM NOT EARTH'S CHAMPION. BESIDES, THE WORLD HAS BROUGHT ME NOTHING BUT PAIN, WAR AND DEATH.
BEHIND YOU IS A DOOR. IF YOU WALK THROUGH IT, YOU WILL BE RETURNED TO THE PHYSICAL WORLD.
IF THE WORLD IS DESTROYED, YOU WILL HAVE NO PEOPLE TO PROTECT.
AND WHAT MAKES YOU THINK THAT CONCERNS ME?
BECAUSE YOU ARE THE SAME WARRIOR WHO HALTED THE MARCH OF HER ENTIRE ARMY TO SAVE ONE HELPLESS CHILD.
YOUR BLADE IS TRULY AS POWERFUL AS YOU SAY IT IS?
YES. BUT THIS IS NOT JUST ABOUT USEH'S DANGER TO THE WORLD. YOU NEED IT TO SAVE AZZAZ AS WELL. I JUST NEED YOU TO TRUST ME.

VERY WELL. WHAT MUST I DO?
TO WIELD DRAGON'S DESTINY IN THE PHYSICAL WORLD, YOU MUST FIRST PASS THE DRAGON TRIALS IN HERE.
IT WAS NOT ENOUGH THAT YOUR SPIRIT CHOSE ME?
NO. MY FATHER DESIGNED THE TRIALS TO FIND THE ONE WHO POSSESSES TRUE COURAGE AND UNPARALLELED INTELLECT. THE PERFECT WARRIOR.
THERE ARE FOUR LEVELS. EACH WITH A DIFFERENT DRAGON YOU MUST DEFEAT.
SEEMS STRAIGHTFORWARD ENOUGH.
NO ONE HAS EVER PASSED THE TRIALS. AND SHOULD YOU DIE HERE, YOU DIE IN THE PHYSICAL WORLD.
THE BODY CANNOT EXIST WITHOUT THE MIND.
UNDERSTOOD.
CALM. DESPITE THE ODDS AGAINST YOU.
ROOAARRR
I HAVE ACCOMPLISHED FEATS WHERE ALL BEFORE ME FAILED. I BELIEVE THIS WILL BE NO DIFFERENT.

YOUR FIRST CHALLENGE IS YAO. THE WIND DRAGON. OR AS SHE IS COMMONLY REFERRED TO, THE QUEEN OF AIR.
HER ABILITY TO MANIPULATE THE WIND GIVES HER INCREDIBLE SPEED. SHE ALSO HEALS AT A REMARKABLE RATE.
TWOOOM
SWOOOM!!

DO YOU SEE IT, FATHER? HER INSTINCTS ARE IMPECCABLE.
THEY ARE. WE SHALL SEE IF SHE TRULY IS THE PERFECT WARRIOR.
FATHER, I KNOW THEY HAVE DONE PLENTY TO ABUSE YOUR FAITH IN THEM, BUT PLEASE, GIVE HER A CHANCE.
VERY WELL.
WHOOM
RAARH!!!

MY INSTINCTS... THEY FEEL...
BATTLES THAT TAKE PLACE IN THE PHYSICAL ARE OFTEN WON FIRST IN THE MIND. THAT IS WHY YOU ARE ALWAYS ONE STEP AHEAD OF YOUR FOES.
I FEEL STRONGER... PHYSICALLY.
THE BLADE GIVES YOU *DIVINE POWER*. SHOULD YOU PASS THE TRIALS, YOU WILL HAVE THE SAME POWERS IN THE PHYSICAL WORLD.
IN HERE, YOU ARE LIMITED ONLY BY YOUR MENTAL CAPACITY. YOU ARE WHAT YOU THINK. THIS IS WHY SO MANY HAVE FAILED THE TRIALS. YOU MORTALS HAVE NO IDEA THE POWER OF THE MIND. BUT I SUSPECT YOU ARE DIFFERENT.
WHY IS IT SO IMPORTANT TO STOP USEH?
DRAGON'S DOOM HAS ITS OWN SOURCE OF INCREDIBLE POWER. *RAGE*.
IF MY BROTHER'S RAGE IS NOT CONTAINED AT THIS EARLY STAGE, IT WILL SPREAD FROM THE ONE WHO CURRENTLY WIELDS HIS BLADE TO THE ENTIRE WORLD.
AND IN THE CENTURIES TO COME, THERE WILL BE DEADLY WARS BETWEEN A HOST OF NATIONS, GENOCIDE, OPPRESSION, AVARICE, AND INCOMPREHENSIBLE TERROR.
YOU DEFEATED HIM BEFORE. WHY NOT FIGHT HIM AGAIN?
AN EXCELLENT QUESTION. ONE I WILL ANSWER SHOULD YOU PASS THE NEXT TEST.

KRACKAKAA
KRACKAKAA
KRACKAKAA
ARRRR
BEHOLD, MOJA, THE MOTHER OF OCEANS.
MOJA IS BLESSED WITH THE ABILITY TO EXPLOIT THE WAVES OF THE SEA. SHE IS THE SMALLEST OF ALL THE DRAGONS BUT THE MOST CUNNING.
HER HEIGHTENED SENSES MAKE HER REFLEXES SECOND TO NONE.
SO--
TRAP ME IN MY MIND AND THEN VANISH WHEN I HAVE QUESTIONS.
HOW NOBLE.

NOT WILLING TO LEAVE YOUR POSITION OF STRENGTH? SMART.
AHHR!
YAHH!
RRAHH!
RAAH!
HAAA!

SHE HAS AN EXCEPTIONAL MIND.
YES, FATHER. SHE TRULY DOES.
ARGHHH!
VVHAASSHHH
SHE HAS MANAGED TO OUTTHINK THE SHREWDEST OF CREATURES.

BIG MISTAKE!
KOOM

INTENTIONALLY EXHAUSTING YOURSELF TO LURE MOJA AWAY FROM THE WATER. EXCEPTIONAL. BUT HOW WILL YOU PASS THE REST OF THE TRIALS IN SUCH A WEAKENED STATE?
I AM ONLY EVER CONCERNED WITH THE BATTLE AT HAND, THE NEXT BATTLE WILL WORRY ABOUT ITSELF. EACH BATTLE HAS ENOUGH TROUBLE OF ITS OWN.
WELL SAID. BUT IT GETS HARDER FROM HERE.
I WOULD NOT EXPECT ANY LESS. BUT FIRST, YOU PROMISED ME ANSWERS.
THESE MAGNIFICENT CREATURES YOU FIGHT WERE CREATED TO PROTECT HUMANITY. FROM THEIR ESSENCE, DRAGON'S DESTINY WAS FORGED.
A BLADE I WOULD GO ON TO EARN AFTER YEARS OF EXCELLENCE IN MY FATHER'S EYES. THIS DROVE USEH MAD WITH RAGE.
AND THEN HE KILLED YOUR FATHER.
DO NOT BELIEVE EVERYTHING YOU READ...
ONCE USEH CRAFTED DRAGON'S DOOM, WAR WAS INEVITABLE. HE RECRUITED MANY WHO SHARED HIS AFFINITY FOR RAGE AND HATRED.
AND THEN THE CREATURES THAT WERE CREATED TO PROTECT BECAME INSTRUMENTS OF BLOODSHED.
BUT YOU WON. YOU DESTROYED USEH.
DEFEATED, YES. DESTROYED, NO. I TRAPPED MY BROTHER FOR ETERNITY WITHIN DRAGON'S DOOM. SEPARATING HIS SPIRIT FROM HIS BODY.
WHICH IS STILL ON EARTH...
AFTER THE DRAGON WARS, TO PREVENT THE ABUSE OF THEIR POWERS, I SACRIFICED MYSELF IN ORDER TO TRANSFORM AND CONCEAL EACH DRAGON'S ESSENCE INTO SEPARATE STONES.
SO WITHOUT YOUR PHYSICAL FORM, USEH WILL HAVE DOMINION OVER OUR WORLD ONCE HE HAS GATHERED ENOUGH POWER.
YES... BUT WITH MY SPIRIT, YOU CAN HAVE DOMINION OVER HIM.

AM I TRULY TO BELIEVE THAT NO ONE ELSE HAS PASSED THESE TRIALS?
ONE CAME CLOSE...
WHO?
PASS THIS LEVEL AND YOU WILL HAVE YOUR ANSWER.
WHO IS NEXT?
DWOOM
GANSO, THE SHOCK BEHEMOTH.
EASILY THE STRONGEST OF HIS KIN, GANSO HAS THE ABILITY TO GENERATE LIGHTNING.
WELL, SHALL WE?
CAREFUL. HE CAN BE VERY TEMPERAMENTAL.
I AM COUNTING ON IT!
YAAH!

TWOOM
TWOOM
SKRTWOOM
ARGHHH!
ERRR...
SKRK
RAK
KRAKA

SKRRHIIISH
RRRGHHH...
SHE IS WEARY.
YET SHE IS STILL IN CONTROL.
SHE ALWAYS IS.
AARHH!
RRR...

ROARR
GOOD.
SKRRHTTSH
HAVE I VEXED YOU?
IS THAT YOUR BEST?!
YES... ATTACK AT FULL POWER.

ARGGGHHHHHH!
SPLITT
HAAAAA!
URRGH...
CAN YOU FINISH?
I CAN. BUT FIRST, YOU OWE ME ANSWERS.
YOU MENTIONED THERE WAS ONE WHO ALMOST COMPLETED THE TRIALS?
YES. MY BROTHER.

USEH TOOK THE TRIALS?
AS I SAID EARLIER, DO NOT BELIEVE EVERYTHING YOU READ.
HISTORY RECORDS TWO BROTHERS. BUT THERE WAS A THIRD.
WHO?
THAT I CANNOT ANSWER.
CANNOT? OR WILL NOT?
BOTH. NOW, I SUGGEST YOU CONSERVE WHAT ENERGY YOU HAVE LEFT TO FACE YOUR FINAL CHALLENGE. THE IBEJI.
IBEJI?
TWIN DRAGONS.
I THOUGHT I WAS FIGHTING ONE DRAGON AT EACH LEVEL?
THE IBEJI ARE CONSIDERED ONE SOUL CONTAINED IN TWO DRAGONS. GANJU CONTROLS FIRE, OKUN, FROST. THE IBEJI'S NEAR UNBREAKABLE SKIN MAKE THEM A MOST FORMIDABLE FOE.

SHE ASKED ABOUT OLON?
YES. DO YOU EVERY REGRET IT? CASTING HIM OUT AS A *JIN*?
OF COURSE. BANISHING MY OWN SON BROUGHT ME NOTHING BUT PAIN. BUT IT HAD TO BE DONE.
I KNOW THE BURDEN LEFT BEHIND BY BOTH YOUR BROTHERS' FAILURES ARE GREAT. AS A FATHER, I COULD NOT HAVE WISHED FOR A BETTER SON TO CARRY IT.
AS A SON, I COULD NOT HAVE WISHED FOR A BETTER FATHER. I CARRY THE BURDEN WITH PRIDE.
HAAAAAA!
SHE DOES NOT SEEM TO HAVE VERY MUCH LEFT.
THAT IS WHEN SHE IS AT HER BEST.
THEIR HIDE IS TOO THICK. I CANNOT PENETRATE IT.
WORSE, I CAN BARELY STAND. I NEED TO END THIS BATTLE QUICKLY. BUT HOW?
WHAT WOULD *NADIA* DO?
NADIA. OF COURSE.
BOTH OF YOU REMIND ME OF MY SISTER AND I.
AS YOUNG WARRIORS, NADIA AND I WERE AN UNSTOPPABLE *TEAM*.

THE ONLY TIME WE EVER LOST WAS TO THE ENEMY WHO MANAGED TO PIT US AGAINST EACH OTHER.
SHOORRRR
FRRZZZZ
WE DID THE WORK FOR THEM.
BHOOM

SHE DID IT.
YES, SHE DID. NOW COMES THE TRUE TEST. WILL SHE STAY THE COURSE AFTER HER BLOCKED MEMORIES ARE RESTORED?
TIME TO FIND OUT.
SO, THIS IS WHAT IT FEELS LIKE.
YOU ARE THE FIRST MORTAL TO WIELD DRAGON'S DESTINY.
THE FIRST TO HARNESS *DIVINE POWER*.
NOW I MUST TEND TO MY PEOPLE. AZZAZ IS IN DANGER. I CAN FEEL IT NOW MORE THAN EVER.
ANY FINAL WORDS OF WISDOM?
YES YOU MUST. AS BEFORE, THE DOOR BEHIND YOU WILL RETURN YOU TO THE PHYSICAL WORLD.
YOU MENTIONED YOU WERE NOT EARTH'S CHAMPION. THE TRIALS HAVE PROVED OTHERWISE.
REMEMBER, THE WORLD IS MUCH BIGGER THAN YOUR IMMEDIATE PROBLEMS.
I MUST NOW RESTORE YOUR MEMORIES. DO NOT LET YOUR TRAUMA OVERCOME YOU. YOU MUST STAY FOCUSED AND REMEMBER YOUR MISSION.
UNDERSTOOD.

NO!!
THEY TOOK EVERYTHING AWAY FROM ME!
MALIKA! YOU MUST CALM YOURSELF. YOUR MIND IS COLLAPSING. IF YOU DIE, THIS WOULD ALL HAVE BEEN FOR NOTHING. FOCUS!
KROOOM
THEY TOOK... THEY TOOK EVERYTHING.
REMEMBER, USEH IS THE REAL THREAT. DO NOT ALLOW HIS RAGE CONSUME THE EARTH.
IT IS NOT USEH'S RAGE THE WORLD NEEDS TO FEAR. IT IS MINE!
FATHER.
FEAR NOT. WHEN THE TIME COMES, SHE WILL RISE TO THE OCCASION.

ARGGHH!
CITY OF CONFLUENCE, AZZAZ.
MNRGH...
MALIKA!
NO!
I AM SORRY.
SLIINN!
THE EN

WINDMAKER™

"Birth of a King"

Creator and Writer
Roye Okupe

Art **Sunkanmi Akinboye**

Colors **Tarella Pablo**

Letters **Bode Joseph**

Cover Art (previous page)
and Concept Art
Godwin Akpan

BONUS STORY—UNIQUE TO THIS EDITION!

YOU'RE RIGHT, SIR. SORR--I MEAN, YES, SIR.

AREN'T YOU SUPPOSED TO BE ON YOUR WAY TO A CABINET MEETING?

YES. BUT I WANTED TO GET SOME AIR BEFORE THE PEOPLE I SELECTED TO ADVISE ME HINT AT HOW TERRIBLE A JOB THEY THINK I'M DOING AS ***PRESIDENT***.

KING BASS. THE LEGENDARY ***WINDMAKER***.

"I WILL GIVE MY LAST BREATH TO PRESERVE THE BEAUTY OF THIS GREAT KINGDOM."
YOU'VE ALWAYS BEEN SO FASCINATED WITH HIM. MORE SO THAN EVEN THE **SAGES**. WHY?

I DON'T KNOW. I JUST FEEL A CONNECTION.

SO...WHAT'S YOUR FAVORITE STORY ABOUT THE "GREAT" KING?
YOUR EXCELLENCY, I'D HATE TO BORE YOU WITH--

TRUST ME, SON. YOU'D BE DOING ME A FAVOR. I NEED A DISTRACTION FROM OUR...CURRENT SITUATION.
OKAY, SIR.

FOR ME, IT HAS TO BE THE BATTLE AT ***OMINIRA***.
AH... THE GENESIS OF THE GREAT REVOLUTION.

PEOPLE THINK BASS BECAME KING AFTER HE DROVE AWAY THE ROGUE MING GENERAL, CHENG.
BUT BASS BECAME KING THE MOMENT HE WITNESSED THE DEATH OF THE ANCIENT ELDERS.

"I CAN ONLY IMAGINE THE HORROR...

"SEEING THE PEOPLE YOU LOVED AND LOOKED TO FOR GUIDANCE, SLAUGHTERED...

"...BY A MAN WHO WENT AGAINST EVERYTHING HIS OWN PEOPLE STOOD FOR.

"TO HONOR OUR FALLEN HEROES, BASS NAMED THE GROUP THAT WOULD FIGHT FOR FREEDOM AND JUSTICE THE *RED RAVENS*.
"'FOR THESE BIRDS NOW CARRIED THE SOULS OF THE MARTYRS.'

"AND SO BEGAN THE *REVOLUTION*. BUT NOT WITHOUT HELP FROM AN UNEXPECTED *ALLY*.

"IN THAT MOMENT, A KING WAS BORN."

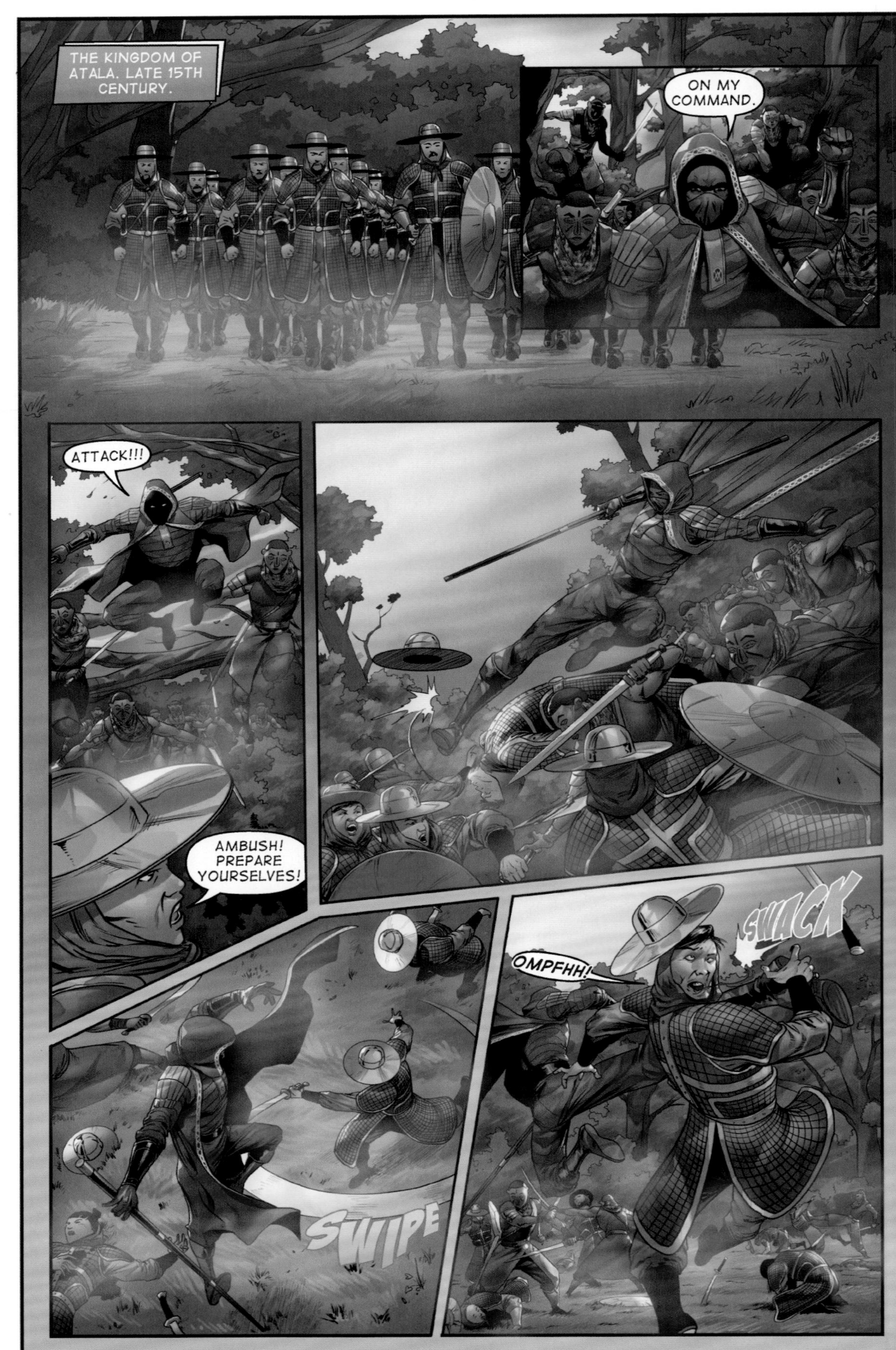
THE KINGDOM OF ATALA. LATE 15TH CENTURY.
ON MY COMMAND.
ATTACK!!!
AMBUSH! PREPARE YOURSELVES!
SWIPE
OMPFHH!
SWACK

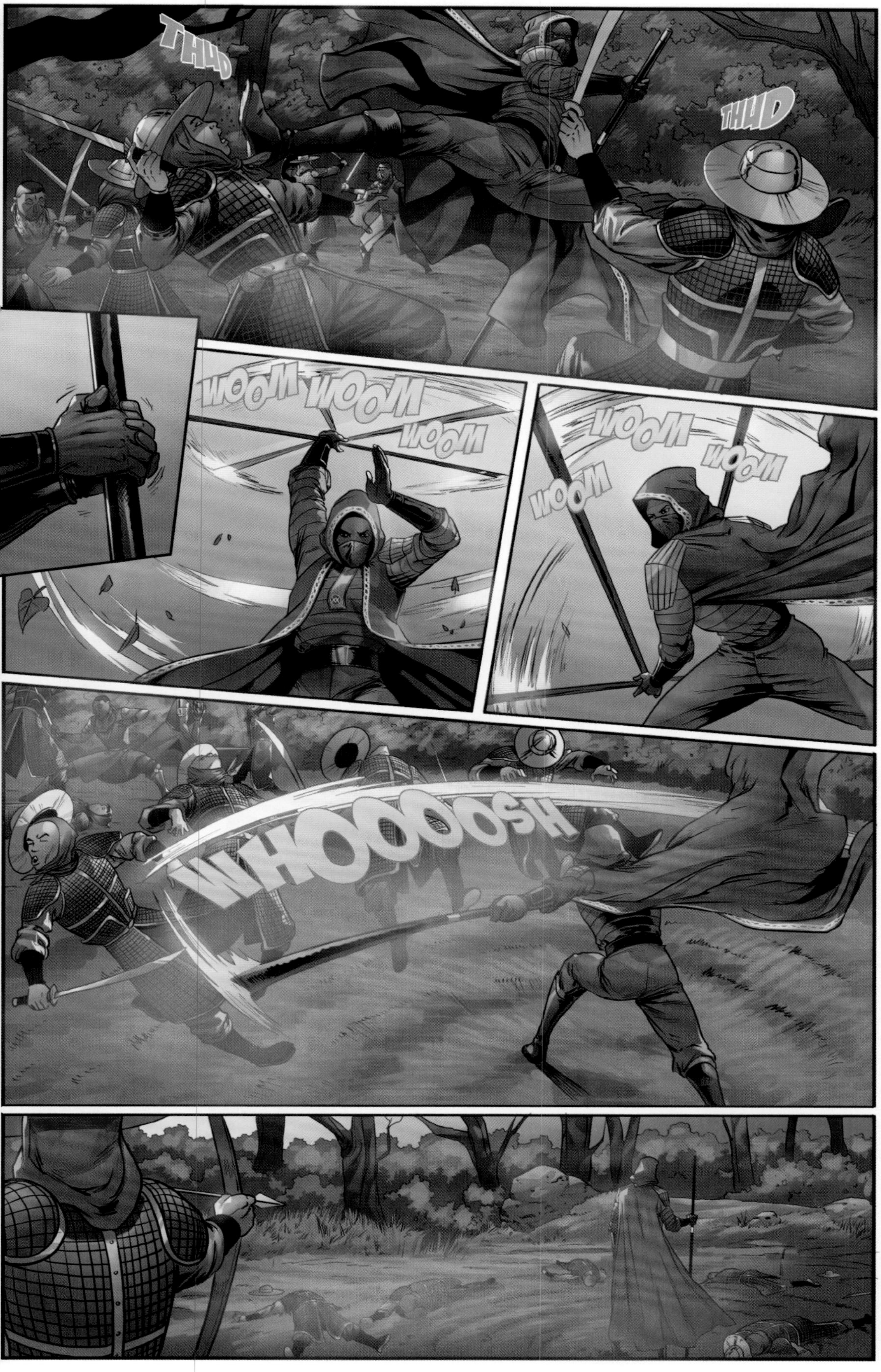

THUD

THUD

WOOM WOOM

WOOM

WOOM

WOOM

WOOM

WHOOOOOSH

TWIP
WHAT?!
THOK
THUD
THUD

MOMENTS LATER.

BASS. COME TO ME.

HORFF

GRRRRRRRRRR

ANOTHER SUCCESSFUL AMBUSH, MY KING.

ANY SIGN OF ZHANG?
NO, MY KING. THE COLONEL WAS NOT LEADING THIS BATTALION.

長将军
BUT WE FOUND THIS. COORDINATES TO A SMALL VILLAGE.
IT HAS ZHANG'S NAME ON IT. IT'S A TWO-DAY JOURNEY.
WE SHOULD STRIKE AS SOON AS POSSIBLE!

COLONEL ZHANG IS THE HEART OF THEIR ARMY. WE REMOVE HIM, AND WE CRIPPLE GENERAL CHENG'S PLANS.
WE CAN FINALLY TURN THE TIDE IN THIS WAR.
AGREED.

MY KING... BASS. WHAT TROUBLES YOU?
THE VISIONS. THEY ARE BECOMING MORE FREQUENT. ALSO...ATALA. HE SPEAKS.

HAVE FAITH, BASS. HAS HE NOT GUIDED US THUS FAR?
IT IS DIFFERENT THIS TIME, BENGU. I CANNOT ABANDON THE MEN.
YOU MAY HAVE TO.
WHY?

BECAUSE WE DO NOT PRAY TO THE ***DIVINE ONES***. ATALA, ORIS, AND THE OTHERS, THEY ARE BUT POWERFUL GUARDIANS SENT BY *AKODA AYE, ASEDA ORUN*.
THE MASTER OF ALL THINGS. THE ONE WE LOOK UP TO. THROUGH THEM, HE SPEAKS.

YOU ARE A GREAT LEADER, BASS. YOU WILL DO THE RIGHT THING.
I NEVER WANTED TO LEAD.
WANT IS NOT A PREREQUISITE TO THE FULFILLMENT OF DESTINY.
WHAT YOU STRUGGLE WITH IS FEAR OF RELINQUISHING CONTROL. CHOOSE FAITH INSTEAD.

VERY WELL. I WILL GO TO ORIS ISLAND TO MEDITATE, IF ONLY TO SHUT YOU UP. TAKE CHARGE WHILE I AM AWAY.
AS YOU WISH, MY KING. WE WILL SEARCH FOR ZHANG AT THE VILLAGE. I WILL TAKE A FEW OF THE RED KNIGHTS SO WE CAN MOVE QUICKLY. THE REST WILL JOIN THE ARMY BACK AT OMINIRA.
BE CAREFUL. LET US REGROUP HERE IN FOUR DAYS.

MING CAMP. SOMEWHERE IN ATALA.

GENERAL CHENG. SIR, I HAVE A REPORT.
SPEAK.
THE ATALIANS ARE PLANNING TO ATTACK COLONEL ZHANG AT THE VILLAGE. THEY TOOK THE BAIT.

GOOD.
THAT MAKES NO SENSE. WHY WOULD THEY THINK I'M THERE? EXCEPT...WHERE ARE THE REST OF THE MEN?
DEAD, COLONEL.
THEIR SACRIFICE SHALL NOT BE IN VAIN. YOU ARE DISMISSED.

THIS IS WHAT WE DO NOW? SACRIFICE OUR OWN MEN TO LURE THE RESISTANCE?!
WE MUST DESTROY THE REBELS AND EXTRACT THE SECRETS OF THESE LANDS FROM THEM. NO MATTER THE COST.
AND YOU WILL STOP QUESTIONING MY METHODS, BOY!
GENERAL. WE WERE SENT HERE TO BUILD A RELATIONSHIP WITH THE ATALIANS. FOSTER TRADE RELATIONS TO ACQUIRE RARE MATERIALS THAT CANNOT BE FOUND ANYWHERE ELSE IN THE WORLD.

INSTEAD, WE KILLED THEIR SAGES AND PROVOKED WAR.
TRADE AND RELATIONS WAS THE *EMPEROR'S* MISSION. I HAVE MINE.

ARE THE *DRAGON STONES* TRULY WORTH ALL THIS?
BOY...THEY ARE WORTH MORE THAN YOU CAN IMAGINE.

OBA TOTO BI A RO* YOU KNOW THE INTENSE PAIN AND GUILT I FEEL WHEN I AM NOT FIGHTING ALONGSIDE MY MEN...MY BROTHERS.
YET YOU HAVE ASKED ATALA TO BRING ME HERE. IN THE MIDDLE OF WAR. WHY?
*A KING WHO IS TRULY WORTHY.
THIS ONCE PEACEFUL PLACE WAS A UTOPIA FOR MY PEOPLE. THE VERY WAR YOU HAVE PULLED ME AWAY FROM HAS TURNED IT INTO A BARREN LAND.
I DOUBT I WILL FIND PEACE OR THE ANSWERS I SEEK HERE. STILL, I WILL TRY.

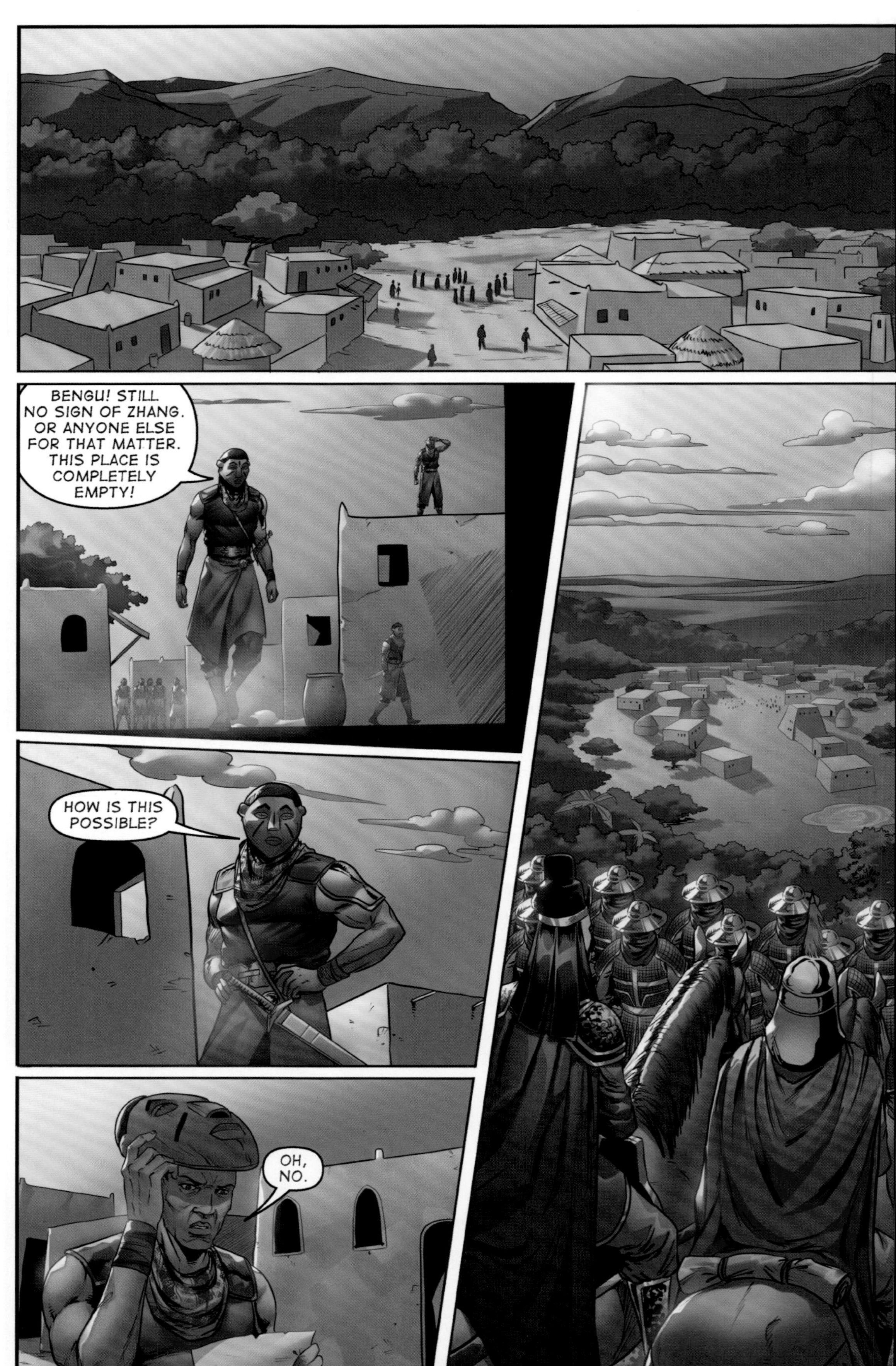
BENGU! STILL NO SIGN OF ZHANG. OR ANYONE ELSE FOR THAT MATTER. THIS PLACE IS COMPLETELY EMPTY!
HOW IS THIS POSSIBLE?
OH, NO.

BEGIN.
ATTACK!
DUWA! QUICKLY! GET A MESSAGE TO KING BASS. WE WILL BUY YOU AS MUCH TIME AS POSSIBLE.
YES, COMMANDER!
THE REST OF YOU, RALLY TO ME!
IF WE ARE TO DIE TODAY...
...WE DO SO DEFENDING OUR FREEDOM!

WHAT DO YOU WANT?!

GRRRRRRRR

RRAAAARR

TWO DAYS. AND STILL YOU ARE SILENT. WHY AM I HERE?! AND WHY WILL YOU NOT SPEAK?!
SHRIEEEK
NO...

MY DESIRE WAS TO BE WITH MY MEN, YET YOU BROUGHT ME HERE! FOR WHAT?! CRYPTIC VISIONS?!
IS YOUR WILL FOR US TO FALL INTO THE HANDS OF THE ENEMY?!
AND WHY DO YOU REMAIN SILENT?! WHY?!
WHY?!!!
FEAR CANNOT COEXIST WITH FAITH
FORGIVE ME. FOR NOW I KNOW YOU STILL SPEAK THROUGH YOUR VESSELS AT ALL TIMES...
...SOMETIMES, NOT IN THE WAY I EXPECT.

GRRRRRRRRR

RRAAAARR

WAKOOOM
WHAT IS HAPPENING?
THE WIND STONE! IT HAS BEEN HERE ALL THIS TIME?!

WHOOOMMF!!
AARGGGHHHHHH!!
RRRGGGHHHHH!

RRRGGHHH...
SEARCH EVERYWHERE! DO NOT LET HIM ESCAPE ELSE CHENG WILL HAVE OUR HEADS!
I AM SORRY, MY KING.

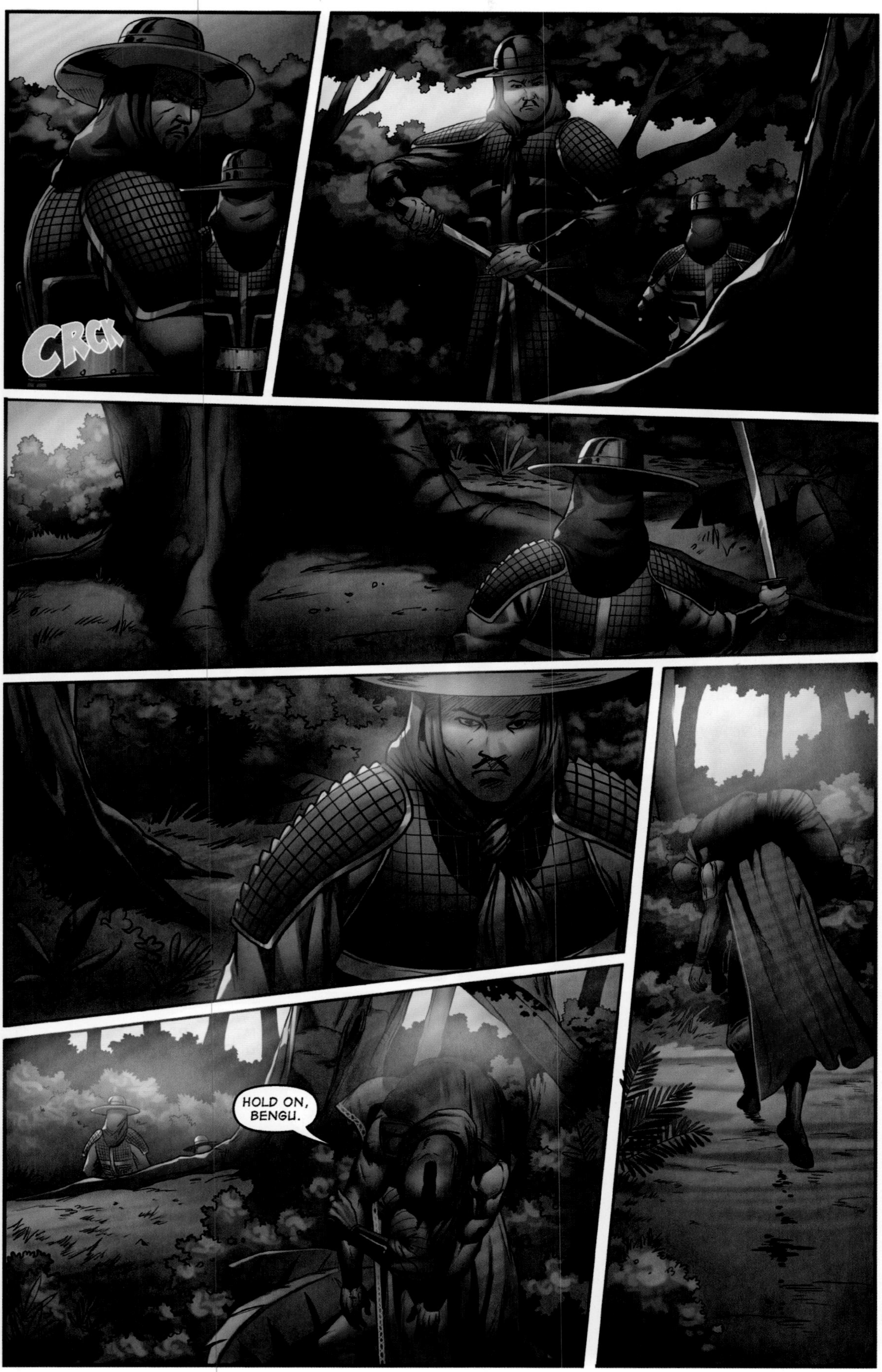

CRCK
HOLD ON, BENGU.

MY KING! WHAT ARE... WHERE ARE WE--?
RELAX, BROTHER. WE ARE SAFE.

EASY, BENGU. YOUR WOUNDS ARE SEVERE. YOU SHOULD BE DEAD.
BUT WE BOTH KNOW YOU ARE MUCH TOO STUBBORN FOR THAT.
WHERE ARE WE?

OMINIRA. ABOUT HALF A DAY'S JOURNEY FROM CAMP.

DID YOU HEAR THAT?

YES. IT WOULD APPEAR THAT WE ARE SURROUNDED.
NOT AGAIN. AND WHY ARE YOU SO CALM?!

MY KING, YOU SHOULD HAVE LEFT ME. YOU ARE FAR MORE IMPORTANT TO THIS WAR THAN ANY ONE OF US.
I WILL HOLD THEM OFF WHILE YOU ESCAPE. QUICKLY! RETREAT!
KING BASS, YOU ARE SURROUNDED!
SURRENDER IMMEDIATELY OR WE WILL KILL YOU.
MY KING, PLEASE! LET ME DO THIS. YOU SAID IT YOURSELF, I SHOULD BE DEAD ALREADY.
THIS REVOLUTION WILL NOT LAST WITHOUT YOU! YOU ARE MORE IMPORTANT THAN ANY ONE OF US. PLEASE!
NOW WHO LACKS FAITH?
WHAT?!
LAST WARNING! SURRENDER OR PERISH!
BENGU, LOWER YOUR BLADE AND GET BEHIND ME.
BENGU!
BUT MY KING, I--
CHARGE!

WHOOOOSH
KRAAAK
WAAAM
THE POWER OF YAO! THE SAGES WERE CORRECT! HE IS THE CHOSEN ONE.
WE FOUND THEM!

ALL HAIL THE KING!
ALL HAIL KING BASS!
RISE. ALL OF YOU.

I AM HONORED BY YOUR PRAISE. EVEN MORE HONORED THAT YOU CHOSE ME AS YOUR KING. BUT YOUR REVERENCE IS NOT WHAT I SEEK. INSTEAD, I ASK HUMBLY FOR YOUR COURAGE. YOUR WILL. YOUR STRENGTH.
TODAY WE SCORED A HUGE VICTORY, BUT THE BATTLES TO COME WILL NOT BE EASY.
THE ENEMY IS WELL TRAINED, DEVIOUS, AND DISCIPLINED. WORST OF ALL, THEY OUTNUMBER US TEN TO ONE.
BUT FEAR NOT. FOR ATALA, ORIS, AND ALL THE *DIVINE ONES* ARE WITH US! AND WITH THEM, WE WILL RECLAIM EVERYTHING THE ENEMY HAS STOLEN FROM US!

TO VICTORY!!!
FOR ATALA!!!!

BENGU. THANK YOU FOR HELPING ME FIND MY WAY.
ALWAYS, MY KING.
EVEN WITH THE POWER OF YAO, I FEAR WE CANNOT WIN THIS WAR ALONE. WE NEED *ALLIES*.

WHO?

WE MUST LOOK NORTH.
YOU MEAN THE AZZAZIANS? *QUEEN MALIKA?*
YES.

PRESENT DAY.
AND THUS A KING WAS BORN.
THAT STORY NEVER GETS OLD.
WOW! SEEMS WE BOTH GOT CARRIED AWAY. I'M LATE FOR MY CABINET MEETING.
APOLOGIES, YOUR EXCELLENCY.
AGAIN WITH THE APOLOGIES. O KIN GBORO.*
*YOU DON'T LISTEN.
STILL WORKING ON THAT, YOUR EXCELLENCY.
GOOD. ANY ADVICE FOR ME AS I WALK INTO THE LION'S DEN?
IT IS NOT MY PLACE TO GIVE ADVICE, SIR. NEITHER DO I HAVE THE REQUIRED WISDOM.
WELL, YOU HAVE TO. BECAUSE THAT WAS NOT A REQUEST.
OKAY, SIR.
WELL...PERHAPS IT WILL BE BENEFICIAL TO DELEGATE RESPONSIBILITY AND EMPOWER YOUR CABINET MORE.
IT WILL HELP WITH THE PUBLIC PERCEPTION OF YOU BEING A "DICTATOR."
AFTER ALL, ISN'T THAT WHAT A DEMOCRACY IS? POWER TO THE PEOPLE? OR AM I WRONG?
YOU HAVE MUCH TO LEARN, MY DEAR BOY. DEMOCRACY IS NOT FOR EVERY NATION. REAL LIFE IS VERY DIFFERENT FROM THE FANTASIES OF THE OLD KINGDOM.
AND I COULD CARE LESS ABOUT WHAT PEASANTS THINK OF ME.

WE WANT REAL DEMOCRACY!
SAY NO TO DICTATORS!
NO MORE CORRUPTION!!
THE END...WANT MORE?